Hunting Cockroaches

Hunting Cockroaches and Other Plays

JANUSZ GŁOWACKI

Northwestern University Press   Evanston, Illinois

Northwestern University Press
Evanston, Illinois 60201

Printed in the United States of America

The paper used in this publication meets the minimum
requirements of American National Standard for Information
Sciences—Permanence of Paper for Printed Library Materials,
ANSI Z39.48-1984

Library of Congress Cataloging-in-Publication Data

Głowacki, Janusz.
  Hunting cockroaches and other plays / Janusz Głowacki.
    p.   cm.
  Translated from the Polish.
  Contents: Cinders — Hunting cockroaches — Fortinbras gets
    drunk.
  ISBN 0-8101-0868-2. — ISBN 0-8101-0869-0 (pbk.)
  1. Głowacki, Janusz—Translations, English.   I. Title.
PG7166.L58A24   1990
891.8'527—dc20
                                         90-34298
                                            CIP

Contents

Cinders

CHARACTERS

Inspector	Father
Principal	First Ugly Sister
Deputy	Second Ugly Sister
Cinderella	Director
Prince	Electrician
Fairy Godmother	Cameraman
Mouse	Soundman
Stepmother	Clappergirl

The action takes place in a girls' reform school somewhere in Poland. Not that far from Warsaw, really.

ACT ONE   Scene 1

[*Typical boarding school recreation room. Tables, chairs, magazines. A closed piano. Only the heavily barred windows suggest this is not an ordinary room. From another room a song can be heard, sung by a chorus of girls. Two men enter: the* PRINCIPAL *of the girls' reform school, and the* INSPECTOR. *Both have intelligent faces (we learn more later). They sit at one of the tables. Singing continues in an adjoining room.*]

GIRLS. I'M FROM A RESPECTABLE HOME.
     I NEVER MEET BOYS ON THE QUIET.
     I NEVER GO OUT ON MY OWN.
     MY FOLKS WOULDN'T DARE LET ME
          TRY IT.
INSPECTOR. Well, yes! Indeed! Very nice.
PRINCIPAL. Thank you.
INSPECTOR. Singing lesson?
PRINCIPAL. Singing lesson.
GIRLS. I NEVER GO OUT ON MY OWN.
     I'VE NEVER BEEN OUT ON A DATE.
     MY PARENTS STILL KEEP ME AT HOME
     AND GIVE ME SWEETS AND CHOCO-
          LATE CAKE.
INSPECTOR. What kind of song is that?
PRINCIPAL. It's one of their favorites.
INSPECTOR. Young people certainly are imaginative.

3

Charming, very charming. But that's not what I want to talk about. A film director wants to make a film about your school, focusing on the play your girls are doing.

PRINCIPAL. *Cinderella?*

INSPECTOR. *Cinderella.*

PRINCIPAL. What do you think about it?

INSPECTOR. Well, you can be proud that he chose your school. No good film has ever been made about this kind of institution.

PRINCIPAL. I know that.

INSPECTOR. The whole country will watch this film about your school and your girls.

PRINCIPAL. I understand.

INSPECTOR. Are you sure you do?

PRINCIPAL. No I don't.

GIRLS. [*singing*] I DON'T FANCY SWEETS ANY-
WAY.
I WANT SOMEONE TO LOVE ME
INSTEAD.
WON'T SOMEBODY TAKE ME
AWAY?
I'M SICK OF THE SWEETS I'M
FED.

INSPECTOR. Yes, very nice. Look, we're living in the twentieth century. Film cameras can go anywhere. Our institution is state run. Everything here is in the open. We have nothing to hide.

PRINCIPAL. No.

INSPECTOR. At the same time, there is no reason to open our doors to the whole country. We can go ahead with this film, showing our courage in openly revealing the more . . . difficult aspects of school life. On the other hand, there is no reason to leave unexamined the more cheerful side of life here. I would never dream of encouraging you to agree to the idea of this film. At the same time, I would be the last person to discourage you. Let's not beat around the bush. Why don't you give your consent? Or, alternately, why not refuse your consent? Withhold cooperation.

GIRLS. HOORAY IT'S MY BIRTHDAY TODAY!
THIS DAY I SHALL NEVER FORGET.
MY FAMILY'S ALL COMING TO STAY.
JUST THINK OF THE PRESENTS I'LL
GET!

INSPECTOR. I can guarantee you one thing, you'll have the inspectorate's full support. But let me advise you that we'll be keeping a watchful eye every step of the way.

PRINCIPAL. Thank you very much.

INSPECTOR. Please don't mention it. Well, that's our official position and we'll stand by it.

GIRLS. OH LOOK AT THE GOODIES I'VE
GOT—
CHOCOLATES AND MARZIPAN!
BUT ALL I CAN SAY IS *SO WHAT*?
I'LL SHOUT IT AS LOUD AS I CAN
THAT I DON'T WANT MORE SWEETS
ANYWAY.
I WANT SOMEONE TO LOVE ME IN-
STEAD.
WON'T SOMEBODY TAKE ME AWAY?
I'M SICK OF THE SWEETS I'M FED.

INSPECTOR. Listen, tell you what. Why don't we have a talk? Confidentially, I like you. I know you want to distinguish yourself. But I'm curious to know—in confidence, now—what on earth possessed you to put on a play as stupid as this fairy tale about—what's her name again?—in a place like this?

PRINCIPAL. Cinderella.

INSPECTOR. Exactly.

PRINCIPAL. It's because I'm unlucky . . .

INSPECTOR. I see.

PRINCIPAL. I always hated sports. You know, running, jumping. I liked peace and quiet. I loved books. But I soon realized that reading gets you nowhere. My friends who played sports were given apartments, bought cars, traveled. If you want to know the truth, I was a pretty good athlete. Once I put the shot a yard further than guys who had been training for a couple of years. I liked teaching. You know, kids. And I didn't do too badly. I got a job in a really good middle school. Appointed vice-deputy head. I was respected.

INSPECTOR. Really?

PRINCIPAL. Yes. They published my articles in educational journals. Then one day, in front of an inspector, the Head asked if anyone had any suggestions—improvements for the school. I began to speak. My colleague, a geography teacher, hit me in the ribs. Apparently the Head wasn't really expecting any suggestions, but I had plenty so I volunteered a few all the same. The Head thanked me profusely, and almost immediately I was appointed head of this reform school. Not that far from Warsaw, really. But I was still full of initiative. That was my problem. So I thought the only way to correct this was to do something I couldn't care less about.

That's when I thought of this play. If there's anything I hate more than sports, it's the theater. And I find the story of Cinderella particularly attractive, since it is utterly devoid of any sense. It's completely meaningless . . . total garbage.

INSPECTOR. I see. And how did that film director hear about it?

PRINCIPAL. I have no idea.

INSPECTOR. You know what? Maybe I shouldn't say this . . . but I sincerely hope you come out of this in one piece.

PRINCIPAL. Thank you so much. What a kind thought. You know, I . . .

INSPECTOR. Go on.

PRINCIPAL. It's nothing. It's just that no one has ever wished me well before.

INSPECTOR. In that case, I'll admit to you—in confidence of course—between the two of us—

PRINCIPAL. Of course!

INSPECTOR. I can't stand the theater either.

PRINCIPAL. I'm so pleased.

INSPECTOR. Can't stand it. But most of all I can't bear those avant-garde plays without intermissions. I prefer your traditional theater—Ibsen, Shakespeare—then you can slip away discreetly after the first act. But with these modern plays you have to sneak up the aisles or sit till the end. Take a masterpiece like *Hamlet*! The first act is quite short. *A Doll's House* is not too bad either.

[*The door opens and* CINDERELLA *looks in. Seeing the* PRINCIPAL *and the* INSPECTOR, *she hesitates a moment, then starts to back out.*]

PRINCIPAL. Come on in. Say hello. [CINDERELLA *executes something between a bow and a curtsy.*]

CINDERELLA. Good morning, Inspector.

INSPECTOR. Good morning.

PRINCIPAL. This is our star.

INSPECTOR. I'm delighted. I'm sorry. What do you mean exactly?

PRINCIPAL. You know. She's playing the lead. In—

INSPECTOR. *Cinderella?*

PRINCIPAL. Yes. Why aren't you in class?

CINDERELLA. I've got to wash my hair.

PRINCIPAL. Now?

CINDERELLA. My teacher said to do it now, so I'll be ready for hairstyling. I'm going to have my hair done. Wanna see the shampoo he gave me?

PRINCIPAL. Ah. What kind is it?

CINDERELLA. Beer.

INSPECTOR. Mmmhmm.

PRINCIPAL. What kind do you use, sir?

INSPECTOR. Egg.

CINDERELLA. Egg? It makes your hair like an omelet.

PRINCIPAL. Lemon and lime is good.

CINDERELLA. Coal tar soap is the best, but I can't get any.

INSPECTOR. Yes, it's true. We haven't solved all our problems. Supplies still aren't up to scratch.

PRINCIPAL. What's your program today?

CINDERELLA. [*in Russian*] Wiecziernaya priczoska.

PRINCIPAL. That means "a day of doing your hair for the evening."

INSPECTOR. Yes, I understand Russian. The girl's accent is excellent. That's good. Education is vital. A grasp of foreign languages, like Russian, broadens one's horizons, allows great intimacy with other cultures and civilizations. Nowadays the world's becoming smaller and smaller. One can be anywhere within a couple of hours. Take advantage of this opportunity to travel. In the old days, children weren't so fortunate. You are very lucky. Well . . . [*Looking at the barred windows, he becomes momentarily confused.*] Are you happy to be in the play? [CINDERELLA *nods.*] Why?

CINDERELLA. I like the theater. [PRINCIPAL *and* INSPECTOR *exchange looks.*]

PRINCIPAL. Off you go. [CINDERELLA *bows and leaves.*]

INSPECTOR. Pretty.

PRINCIPAL. Yes. I suppose she is.

INSPECTOR. And charming.

PRINCIPAL. Yes, she is charming. Yes.

INSPECTOR. What's she here for?

PRINCIPAL. Robbery with violence.

INSPECTOR. Violence?

PRINCIPAL. With a bottle.

INSPECTOR. Amazing. See how deceptive appearances can be? She has the face of—

PRINCIPAL. An angel.

INSPECTOR. Exactly. Who did she use the bottle on?

PRINCIPAL. Her stepfather. So her mother informed us. She stole her stilettos and vanished.

INSPECTOR. Shoes?

PRINCIPAL. Yes.

INSPECTOR. The mother.

PRINCIPAL. The mother.

INSPECTOR. Ah, the mother. Has she been here long?

PRINCIPAL. Two years. She could be released at the end of the year.

INSPECTOR. I wish you luck then. Oh, just one more thing. Will this play of yours have an intermission?

PRINCIPAL. I don't know yet.

INSPECTOR. Hmm. In any case, this time the audience won't be leaving.

Scene 2

[*A professional film crew is setting up camera, lights, directors' chairs, etc.*]

ELECTRICIAN. Did you get a look at them? They're not bad.

CAMERAMAN. They practically shoved their heads through the bars when they saw us coming.

ELECTRICIAN. Not bad at all.

CAMERAMAN. Jesus! You steal, you drink, you screw around, next thing you're a budding film star.

ELECTRICIAN. Jealous?

CAMERAMAN. You gotta be kidding. OK. Let's set up to rehearse.

ELECTRICIAN. I got an idea! If you cut your old lady in half, then someone will film you. Just be scientific about it. Draw a line across her stomach and then . . . chop.

CAMERAMAN. Take it easy.

[*Four* GIRLS *enter carrying a long chest shaped like a coffin. They cover it with a blanket and fix a cross about it. This is the grave of* CINDERELLA'S *mother, where* CINDERELLA *will pray later.*]

ELECTRICIAN. Look at them! Look at them!

[*All the* GIRLS *turn around.* SOUNDMAN *enters. The girl playing the* PRINCE *makes a rude gesture and winks.*]

CAMERAMAN. [*to the* PRINCE] OK, which one of you is supposed to kneel at the grave?

[PRINCE *is sixteen, tall, well built. The* GIRLS *adore her, surround her, blindly obey her.*]

PRINCE. Not me. I'm playing the Prince. Cinderella does the kneeling.

CAMERAMAN. Doesn't matter. You kneel in for her.

PRINCE. For you? I'll kneel down for a butt. One butt, one knee. [*Again, she gestures obscenely and winks at* ELECTRICIAN.]

ELECTRICIAN. I'd give her one. Just like that. Then like that, and then like that.

SOUNDMAN. She's a kid.

ELECTRICIAN. Relax, Pop. She's had more cock than you've had hot dinners.

[*The* PRINCIPAL, *his* DEPUTY, *and the* FILM DIRECTOR *enter in mid-conversation. The* DEPUTY *has a pleasant face, neatly waved black hair; the* DIRECTOR *is blond, impeccably dressed. The* GIRLS, *dazzled, scream in admiration.*]

PRINCIPAL. Mayewsky, it's enough!

DIRECTOR. Good morning, girls. [*approaches and greets them with extreme courtesy*]

PRINCE. [*admiringly*] Check him out!

FAIRY GODMOTHER. Jesus Christ!

DIRECTOR. [*gesturing elegantly at the* GIRLS] You know, I want to protect them. Ask a few questions of society—point the finger a little. How is it possible that young girls—our children—should end up here?

PRINCE. Holy shit. Listen to him talk!

FAIRY GODMOTHER.. He's beautiful.

DIRECTOR. The moment I heard about this play, I thought to myself: this is it. This is an Oberhausen film. What do you think?

DEPUTY. I'm sorry, but I don't speak German.

DIRECTOR. What? Oberhausen. It's a town in West Germany. There's an important film festival there every year.

DEPUTY. Oh. In that case, yes. Certainly, yes.

[*The* SECOND UGLY SISTER *runs in.*]

UGLY SISTER #2. He came in a BMW.

PRINCE. You're kidding.

UGLY SISTER #2. Swear to God.

MOUSE. Well fuck me!

PRINCIPAL. Well, I think you may be a little overhopeful. In any case, a few formalities have to be settled. The parents' consent, for one thing.

DIRECTOR. No problem.

PRINCIPAL. I'm afraid you're right.

FAIRY GODMOTHER. My dad has a Mercedes.

PRINCE. And his prick has wings. [*laughter*]

DIRECTOR. Naturally, we'll pay the parents something for the days we're shooting. That girl has a good face. What part is she playing?

PRINCIPAL. The Prince.

DIRECTOR. Good.

PRINCIPAL. Look, I wonder if . . .

DIRECTOR. Very good. [*walks away*]

UGLY SISTER #2. He's got his eye on you.

PRINCE. Forget it. He's a director. The money's shit and there's no work anyway.

STEPMOTHER. Too bad he's not Polanski.

DIRECTOR. Look, I understand your concern, but it's going to be better if we destroy any illusions right from the start. That's what this film is about!

PRINCIPAL. The girls will have to give their consent.

DEPUTY. That's not a problem.

PRINCIPAL. Of their own free will, Professor.

DEPUTY. Of course, most definitely.

DIRECTOR. So you teach as well?

DEPUTY. Singing, marches, campfire songs. That sort of thing.

DIRECTOR. I'd like to meet the girl who's playing Cinderella.

PRINCIPAL. She's in class now.

DEPUTY. I've always taken an interest in art.

PRINCIPAL. Have you?

DEPUTY. Yes.

PRINCIPAL. Why?

DEPUTY. Because it affords a glimpse of one's higher emotions.

DIRECTOR. Very interesting.

PRINCIPAL. I know you mentioned Oberhausen, but will this film be shown over here too?

DIRECTOR. I hope so.

PRINCIPAL. People will get to know their faces and might remember them later on. That could create problems for the girls.

DIRECTOR. Girls' faces change so quickly at their age.

DEPUTY. Where would they be recognized anyway? Only in criminal circles, where they're known already.

PRINCIPAL. Yes, but they—

DIRECTOR. They're still children. I understand. And that's exactly what we want to show. These children, and I'm not afraid to use the word, have gone through hell. Their experiences are unimaginable to most normal adults like you and me.

PRINCIPAL. Yes, but I still . . .

DEPUTY. Principal, I'm sorry to say this, but you're acting like a child. Their friends will only envy them. As will other people.

[*In the background the lighting rehearsal continues.* ELECTRICIAN #1 *gives a pack of cigarettes to the* PRINCE.]

DIRECTOR. Please, understand. I'm not a sensationalist. Oh, but I have to ask, the thirteen-year-old who stabbed her lover to death with a crochet hook—is she here?

DEPUTY. No.

DIRECTOR. No?

DEPUTY. But there are other interesting ones.

DIRECTOR. But I was going to use her for the title sequence.

DEPUTY. We can do better than that.

DIRECTOR. It doesn't really matter. Maybe it's even better that she's not here. The film will be cleaner. The simple story of an innocent creature caught up in the web of our society—any society. Children, social injustice . . . have you read Dostoevsky?

DEPUTY. Yes. Lovely.

PRINCIPAL. Well. My deputy will take care of you. I have to write some reports. Excuse me, won't you? [*leaving, to* GIRLS] Report to your classes. [GIRLS *exit.*]

DEPUTY. I'm sure you think the Principal's a strange man. I've guessed it, haven't I?

DIRECTOR. Why should I think that?

DEPUTY. I'll tell you in a moment.

DIRECTOR. OK. [*to* CAMERAMAN] How are you doing?

CAMERAMAN. Will you want to go for one hundred percent sound?

SOUNDMAN. We'll never get it clean.

DEPUTY. He has a strange aversion to women.

DIRECTOR. So what? We'll have a full sound rehearsal tomorrow.

SOUNDMAN. I'm still not promising anything.

DEPUTY. It was common knowledge that his wife was happy with him.

DIRECTOR. Well, that's unusual, but not perverse.

DEPUTY. Then one day she poisoned herself. What does one hundred percent sound mean?

DIRECTOR. Live, so we don't have to dub later. So she poisoned herself. So what?

DEPUTY. So you usually have to dub sound afterward? You know, you're right. Who cares if she poisoned herself or not? It happens all the time. But the Public Prosecutor suggested that the Principal attend the autopsy, and he agreed. Well, no wonder he has an aversion to women.

DIRECTOR. We'll need some handheld shots.

CAMERAMAN. What do you want? Close-ups?

DIRECTOR. Sure. [*to* DEPUTY] Can I ask you something?

DEPUTY. I want to ask you something, too. Forgive me, but as I told you, I take a real interest in art. What does handheld mean?

DIRECTOR. Without the tripod.

DEPUTY. Aha, but why? If you've got a tripod?

DIRECTOR. Look, I want to ask you something first. I'm grateful for your help, but why are you telling me all this?

DEPUTY. About the Principal?

DIRECTOR. Yes.

DEPUTY. Because of the way you looked at him.

DIRECTOR. How did I look at him?

DEPUTY. Sort of purposefully. As if you—you know—wanted to know something, but didn't know how to ask. I can read a person like a book.

DIRECTOR. That's great. Tell me, do you think the girls will cooperate?

DEPUTY. Oh, no problem at all. And if worse comes to worst, we'll adopt certain measures . . . sanctions or something.

DIRECTOR. Like what?

DEPUTY. We'll frighten them.

DIRECTOR. How?

DEPUTY. Just . . . gently. For instance, I'll tell them I'll confiscate the TV from their rec room.

DIRECTOR. But there isn't a television in the rec room.

DEPUTY. You're right. We'll have to give them one and then take it away. But this is all hypothetical, of course. Don't worry. Just take it from me. I know how to talk to them. [DEPUTY *rings a bell. The inmates of the school gather for roll call.* PRINCE *gives her report.*]

PRINCE. Number in school: eighty-five. Present: seventy-seven. Four in sick bay, one on leave, three on the run.

DEPUTY. At ease.

PRINCE. [*to* GIRLS] At ease. [*They sit.*]

DEPUTY. As I'm sure you all know already, unofficially, a prominent film director, standing here with me now, is going to make a film in our school. Pride is in order, since no other such institution in this

country can claim this honor. You—that is—
those of you who have been selected—will perform the adventures of one "Cinderella," in ac-
cordance with the original story, while the director
will be filming the performance with a few addi-
tions of his own. From now on, you may consider
yourselves officially informed. The director, like
those of us on the school staff, wants, of course, to
help you. So this film will be shown at home as
well as abroad. Namely in the town of . . . Ub . . .
Ooob . . .

DIRECTOR. Oberhausen.

DEPUTY. Exactly. That's it. My second point: your
participation in this film is entirely voluntary.
Therefore in compliance with the principles of de-
mocracy, I am going to ask you: "Do you want to
take part in the film?" You can then take your cue
from me and reply, "Yes." And I shall be obliged
to reply, "Agreed." Naturally, if this democratic
procedure fails, I shall have to assign you to work
on the film. But I'm sure it won't come to that.
Well now, girls, do you want to take part in the
film?

GIRLS. Yes.

DEPUTY. Dismissed.

DIRECTOR. Thank you.

DEPUTY. Oh, please don't mention it. Simple intu-
ition. You just have to—you know—find the right
psychological key, and then you can count on
them.

DIRECTOR. Who is that girl?

DEPUTY. Which?

DIRECTOR. That one.

DEPUTY. Oh, she's playing the main part.
DIRECTOR. Cinderella?
DEPUTY. That's the one.
DIRECTOR. Good face.
DEPUTY. Quite possibly.

Scene 3

[*Rehearsal in progress.* CAMERAMAN *positions the* GIRLS, *giving them chalk marks on the floor. The* FATHER— *dressed up grotesquely in man's clothing—holds a riding whip in her hand and speaks monotonously. The* UGLY SIS- TERS *are sprawled in their chairs, one painting her nails, the other backcombing her hair. Between them,* CINDER- ELLA, *with her back to the audience, is on her knees clean- ing the floor. In the background are the other* GIRLS *and the* DEPUTY.]

DIRECTOR. All right! Stand by. Going for a take. Lights! [*to* ELECTRICIAN] What kind of focus is that? Could we light the actors, please? Quiet! Roll camera.
CAMERAMAN. Rolling.
SOUNDMAN. Speed.
CAMERAMAN. Mark it, please.

[*The* CLAPPERGIRL *claps the board in front of the* FATHER'*s face.*]

CLAPPERGIRL. Twenty-seven, take one.
DIRECTOR. Action!
FATHER. My dear children, what shall I bring you from the market?
DIRECTOR. Cut! Something's wrong. You have to say that with more feeling. You love them, they're

your children. You want to make them happy. Do you understand? Once again. [*The whole ceremony with the lights, camera, so forth is repeated.*]

CAMERAMAN. Rolling.

SOUNDMAN. Speed.

CAMERAMAN. Mark it, please.

CLAPPERGIRL. Twenty-seven, take two.

DIRECTOR. Action!

FATHER. [*in the same monotone as before*] My dear children, what shall I bring you from the market?

DIRECTOR. Cut. Come here a minute. What are you in here for?

FATHER. Two five seven.

DIRECTOR. What does that mean? [*The* DIRECTOR *signals the* CAMERAMAN *to start shooting.*]

FATHER. Stealing.

DIRECTOR. And what does your father do?

FATHER. Time, mostly.

DIRECTOR. And your mother?

FATHER. She's inside, too.

DIRECTOR. What for?

FATHER. Two five seven.

DIRECTOR. It's a family business.

FATHER. In a way.

DIRECTOR. Do you love your father?

FATHER. Yeah, he's not bad. He always wanted me around when people came to visit. He'd give me a drink or two. In the summer I used to walk with Dad and my uncle to the cornfields. My uncle brought some booze and sausage once. We sat in the corn, drank in the corn, did it all in the corn. First Dad. Then my uncle. Then we played football. My uncle was so drunk, every time he kicked

the ball he fell over. [*long bursts of laughter*] Then
we made daisy chains.

DIRECTOR. And who hurt you the most in your life?

FATHER. No one hurt me.

DIRECTOR. And what do you dream of more than anything else?

FATHER. Working the streets again.

DIRECTOR. Good. Mark it. [*to* CAMERAMAN] OK for
you?

CAMERAMAN. Fine.

SOUNDMAN. OK for me.

CLAPPERGIRL. Twenty-eight, take one, tail slate.

FATHER. [*vacantly*] My dear children, what shall I bring
you from the market?

DIRECTOR. OK. That's good, you can sit down now.
Thank you. Oh, just one more thing. Who in your
life has shown you the most kindness?

FATHER. [*looks toward the* DEPUTY *and recites*] The Deputy Head.

DIRECTOR. [*looks at* DEPUTY, *who smiles humbly*] Yes, I
see. Thank you. Now, First Ugly Sister. Why don't
you come over here and complete a few sentences
for me?

[UGLY SISTER #1 *sits on the chair and freezes with the comb
raised in midair.*]

DIRECTOR. [*continued*] Roll camera.

CAMERAMAN. Rolling.

SOUNDMAN. Speed.

CAMERAMAN. Mark it, please.

CLAPPERGIRL. Twenty-nine, take one.

DIRECTOR. Action! [UGLY SISTER #1 *abruptly starts
combing her hair, then covers her eyes with her hands,*

blinded by the lights.] Wait. What are you squinting for? Go again, same slate.

CAMERAMAN. Rolling.

SOUNDMAN. Speed.

DIRECTOR. My father . . .

UGLY SISTER #1. You're supposed to ask me nice questions. My father beats me. I've got stitches in my head. May I go please? [*She tries to leave.*]

DEPUTY. Sit down. [*She sits.*]

DIRECTOR. OK. The most beautiful day in my life . . .

UGLY SISTER #1. Can't remember.

DIRECTOR. Try.

UGLY SISTER #1. My brother and his friend came to pick me up.

DIRECTOR. Go on.

UGLY SISTER #1. We went to midnight mass. I felt funny and had to go outside. I sat down on a little bench and this friend of my brother's came out. He sat down next to me. He kissed me. We started chasing each other all over the place. Then the police came and picked us up. They let me go but they locked him up.

DIRECTOR. And then what?

UGLY SISTER #1. That's the end of my most beautiful day.

DIRECTOR. All right. Now finish this sentence. Most of all I like . . .

UGLY SISTER #1. Playing with dolls.

DIRECTOR. When I read fairy tales . . .

UGLY SISTER #1. I start to cry.

DIRECTOR. What I'm most frightened of is . . .

UGLY SISTER #1. Getting the clap.

DIRECTOR. Other people . . .

UGLY SISTER #1. Are different.

DIRECTOR. My father . . .

UGLY SISTER #1. Is no different from anyone else.

DIRECTOR. My mother . . .

UGLY SISTER #1. Loves me. [PRINCE *bursts out laughing at this point, and the other* GIRLS *follow suit.*]

DIRECTOR. What is it? What's the matter?

PRINCE. We're jealous. We want a mother like that. [*roars with laughter*]

UGLY SISTER #1. Fuck off!

DIRECTOR. [*whispers to* CAMERAMAN] Stay on her. She's going to cry. [*to* PRINCE] What are you talking about?

PRINCE. When she had pneumonia, her mother got the medicine for nothing on the Health Service. But it just so happened she was very thirsty . . .

DIRECTOR. So what?

PRINCE. You can't drink penicillin, so her Mom swapped it for a bottle. Why d'you wanna cover up for your mother?

UGLY SISTER #1. I'm not covering up for her. She loves me, but she's sick. [DIRECTOR *clasps the* GIRL *to him and strokes her face. She weeps.*]

DIRECTOR. [*after a while*] Cut.

PRINCE. She has to have a drink before breakfast so she won't eat on an empty stomach.

DIRECTOR. That's enough. How was that?

CAMERAMAN. [*gives an OK sign*] Good.

PRINCE. She likes to eat in Chinese restaurants.

DIRECTOR. Why?

PRINCE. Because the cook gives you food he's already chewed up.

UGLY SISTER #1. She's unhappy. That's why she sold it.

But she always bought me everything—jeans, a coat, a watch. [PRINCE *laughs.*]

DIRECTOR. OK, that's enough.

UGLY SISTER #1. She's unhappy. That's why she sold it.

DIRECTOR. Roll it. Who hurt you most in your life?

UGLY SISTER #1. [*looks toward the* DEPUTY *and recites*] Hitler. He shot my father and laughed as he did it.

DIRECTOR. Why?

UGLY SISTER #1. I don't know. It was obviously a necessity of war.

DIRECTOR. And who helped you most in your life?

UGLY SISTER #1. The Deputy Head.

DIRECTOR. [*looks at* DEPUTY *thoughtfully*] Cut! Now, Cinderella.

DEPUTY. Cinderella?

DIRECTOR. Roll camera.

CAMERAMAN. Rolling.

SOUNDMAN. Speed.

CAMERAMAN. Mark it, please.

CLAPPERGIRL. Thirty, take one.

DIRECTOR. Action. The most beautiful moment in my life . . .

CINDERELLA. Talking to you.

DIRECTOR. Thank you very much. What I like most is . . .

CINDERELLA. That's not in the Grimm Brothers' version.

DIRECTOR. OK. OK. Reading fairy tales . . . [CINDERELLA *is silent.*] My father . . . [*She remains silent.*] My mother . . . [*still silent*] Cut.

DEPUTY. Cinderella, don't fool around.

CINDERELLA. I'm not fooling around.

DEPUTY. You are fooling around. And if I say you're

fooling around you are fooling around, even if you aren't fooling around. But you are fooling around. Be careful or you'll go too far.

DIRECTOR. Don't you want to act?

CINDERELLA. Yes, but only in the play. I'm allowed to say what I want, aren't I?

DEPUTY. Is anyone saying you're not? I just want to suggest that you're pushing your luck. You'll regret it.

CINDERELLA. Are you finished? Can I go? I mustn't get upset today. I have a very important sewing lesson. I have to cut a pair of trousers, and if my hands are shaking I'll mess up the material.

DEPUTY. Now I'm speaking to you as your teacher. You trust me, don't you?

CINDERELLA. I knew a teacher once who lived next door. He had an eleven-year-old daughter who jumped out of the window.

DEPUTY. I don't have a daughter.

CINDERELLA. That's OK, it's not about you.

DIRECTOR. Go on.

DEPUTY. Just a minute.

CINDERELLA. The other teacher had a wife and a maid. Then he had a child with the maid—a daughter. The wife and the maid were killed in the war, so he married the daughter, and he had three more daughters with that daughter. He lived with all four of them until one flew out of the window. No one knows why.

DEPUTY. Go on.

CINDERELLA. The end.

DEPUTY. Why are you telling us this story?

CINDERELLA. He was a teacher like you. A professor.

DEPUTY. It's possible he was, but only before socialism.

DIRECTOR. Let's take ten! Clear the set, please.

CAMERAMAN. Save the lights.

DIRECTOR. [*to* DEPUTY] You too, if you don't mind. I
want a word with her alone.

[DEPUTY *thinks he senses an ulterior motive in this. He
winks indulgently at the* DIRECTOR *and exits.* DIRECTOR
and CINDERELLA *are left alone on the stage. For a while
they look at each other in silence.*]

DIRECTOR. [*continued*] Listen. I want to help you.

CINDERELLA. Aren't you frightened someone will walk
in?

DIRECTOR. What do you mean?

CINDERELLA. People have wanted to help me before.
One of my Mom's friends, for example.

DIRECTOR. And?

CINDERELLA. Nothing. It just hurt a little.

DIRECTOR. How old were you?

CINDERELLA. Thirteen.

DIRECTOR. Thirteen?

CINDERELLA. Don't laugh at me. I know I started late.
I know I wasted two good years of my life. How
old were you when you started?

DIRECTOR. Why don't you want to be a part of this
film?

CINDERELLA. I do.

DIRECTOR. You don't want to talk about yourself.

CINDERELLA. I'm not that interesting. I could talk
about Hitler if I had to. Or the Deputy, how he
helped me.

DIRECTOR. You remind me of someone.

CINDERELLA. Who?

DIRECTOR. Myself, ten years ago. You're very smart.

CINDERELLA. Not that smart. I landed up here, didn't I?

DIRECTOR. A mistake.

CINDERELLA. Well how do you know I didn't want to? I'm finishing my education, learning a trade.

DIRECTOR. So you want to be a dressmaker?

CINDERELLA. [*ironically*] Oh, I haven't made up my mind yet. I definitely have a gift for it. It's so difficult to decide. I have a lot of choices, you know. I could also be a hairdresser. One should experiment. Like Gorky, you know? After all, what didn't he try? What's your advice? Hairdressing or dressmaking?

DIRECTOR. You have talent. You should think about acting school.

CINDERELLA. Why bother? There's enough drama here. Last night, for example, the Prince, the Mouse, and the Stepmother screwed Ugly Sister.

DIRECTOR. And?

CINDERELLA. She didn't try to stop them.

DIRECTOR. And you?

CINDERELLA. I'm OK, thanks.

DIRECTOR. Did you help?

CINDERELLA. Her or them? And listen, don't bother informing the Deputy or the Principal, because it would only make things worse for her. Informing was the habit they were trying to cure her of. She's always been like that. The minute her father raped her, she squealed on him. They locked him up; he didn't understand what all the commotion was about. He said he'd been brought up in tough circumstances. He said nobody felt sorry for him, or tried to cover for him, and look, he'd grown up as a decent human being. Shall I continue, or are you asleep?

DIRECTOR. Why didn't she tell me all this?

CINDERELLA. She obviously forgot.

DIRECTOR. Like you.

CINDERELLA. Yeah. Something like that.

DIRECTOR. Don't you want to defend yourself? Don't you want to accuse someone? This film could help you.

CINDERELLA. Don't get sentimental. You think they'll let me out? I've done okay so far, thanks.

DIRECTOR. So?

CINDERELLA. Nothing doing.

DIRECTOR. You're going to fuck up this whole thing.

CINDERELLA. Shame.

DIRECTOR. I can make things very uncomfortable for you.

CINDERELLA. I've heard that before.

DIRECTOR. Why did you attack your stepfather? Hmm? Jealous of your mother? And how was it with your stepfather? Did your mother watch?

[CINDERELLA *raises her arm to hit the* DIRECTOR, *but he ducks fast and smiles. She runs out. Offstage the* GIRLS *are singing.*]

GIRLS. UP THE STAIRS AND IN THE ATTIC
FIND TWO LOVERS SLEEPING.
FAIR-HAIRED LILI WITH HER HERO
DREAMS OF LOVE AND KEEPING.

JIM KNOWS PARIS LIKE HIS POCKET.

OUT HE GOES A-THIEVING.
FAIR-HAIRED LILI IN THE WINDOW
SINGS OF LOVE AND LEAVING.

TINY LILI, SWEET AS HONEY,
TAKE A LOOK AROUND YOU.
ALL OF PARIS AT YOUR FEET
AND HEAVEN ABOVE TO CROWN YOU.

Scene 4

[CINDERELLA *is kneeling at her mother's grave. She prays, her hands covering her face. Suddenly the* FAIRY GOD-MOTHER *appears, dressed in a flowing robe.* CINDERELLA *looks up, leaps to her feet in terror.*]

FAIRY GODMOTHER. Do not fear me, Cinderella. I am
    your Fairy Godmother.
    You have a wicked Stepmother and no other.
    You see I know all about you.
    I shall grant your wish too.
    I have brought you a beautiful dress
    And you shall go to the Prince's ball dressed like a
    princess.

[*From behind her she produces a dress made of colored tissue paper, a paper crown, and a pair of slippers.* CINDER-ELLA *puts them on, then turns to face the camera.*]

DIRECTOR. My mother . . . My stepfather . . . Cut.
    Set up for the next scene please. Stepmother and
    ugly sisters on set. Where are the ugly sisters?

[GIRLS *and* CREW *exit. The* DEPUTY *enters.*]

DEPUTY. How's it coming along?

DIRECTOR. Slowly.

DEPUTY. Why is that?

DIRECTOR. Cinderella . . .

DEPUTY. Fooling around?

DIRECTOR. Yes. Anyway, it's flat. One-dimensional—they have to open up, do you understand? It's lifeless. At this rate, it's just going to be interventionist propaganda. We need a shock, an explosion. I've got to provoke tears, pity, fear.

DEPUTY. Well, they're certainly frightened.

DIRECTOR. I'm talking about Oberhausen. People have to identify. We have to squeeze those bleeding hearts in the West. And Cinderella is perfect. But she won't cooperate.

DEPUTY. Well, we could make things uncomfortable for her, but the Principal wouldn't agree.

DIRECTOR. To hell with the Principal.

DEPUTY. Yes of course. But . . .

DIRECTOR. Listen. We're talking about art! And why are they all obsessed with Hitler? "He shot my father and laughed as he did it."

DEPUTY. What do you object to in that?

DIRECTOR. It's ridiculous! I can't use that. How old are they supposed to have been when they witnessed that?

DEPUTY. Well, I'm sorry, but wasn't that the kind of thing you were looking for . . . for . . . whatever it is . . . you know . . .

DIRECTOR. What?

DEPUTY. Well, Ober . . . you know—?

DIRECTOR. Oberhausen. Yes, maybe from one of them, but not all of them. And what was all that garbage the stepmother was on about blaming her troubles on the Wolski Brothers, who beat her up after she burned down their farm because they belonged to the Wehrmacht!? She said she caught up with them one by one and took revenge on them by poking their eyes out.

DEPUTY. Yes.

DIRECTOR. Where the hell did she get that? That's a man's story, for Chrissake.

DEPUTY. Well, one of the wardens told me that one. It's a good story, I think.

DIRECTOR. There's another thing. Not that important.

DEPUTY. Good.

DIRECTOR. But delicate.

DEPUTY. Ah!

DIRECTOR. I don't know if it's wise to have them all saying that you are the single person in their lives who's done the most to help them.

DEPUTY. Let me be quite candid with you. It's bothered me, too. But after all, you wanted them to be honest. . . . One of those Ugly Sisters went a little overboard I thought, with that story about the sick mother.

DIRECTOR. No. That was very moving. I can use that. And her mother will be happy about it.

DEPUTY. Well, there you are then.

DIRECTOR. But what are we going to do about Cinderella?

DEPUTY. It's really an unpleasant business.

DIRECTOR. Well, think of something. You're the expert.

DEPUTY. [*an idea*] We could replace her!

DIRECTOR. [*ironical*] Thank you. Thank you very

much. [DEPUTY *smiles modestly. To* CREW *and* GIRLS *who have returned to set*] OK, let's go. Stepmother!]

[*The* UGLY SISTERS *are lying on a table, covered by a sheet. They sit up in unison, whisper something, then lie down again. This is repeated several times.* STEPMOTHER *stands beside them in curlers.*]

STEPMOTHER. My dear sweet daughters, it's morning. What shall I bring you for breakfast?

UGLY SISTERS #1 & #2. [*together*] Oh Mama, you are so kind!

DIRECTOR. OK, lights please. Let's go for a take. For God's sake. Quiet, please. Roll the camera.

CAMERAMAN. Rolling.

SOUNDMAN. Sound running.

DIRECTOR. And . . . action.

STEPMOTHER. My dear sweet daughters, it's morning. What shall I bring you for breakfast?

UGLY SISTER #1. [*together*] Oh Mama, you are so good!

UGLY SISTER #2. [*together*] Oh Mama, you are so kind!

DIRECTOR. What's the matter with you two?

UGLY SISTER #2. It's supposed to be "kind." She fucked up.

UGLY SISTER #1. It's "good!"

UGLY SISTER #2. It's "kind!"

UGLY SISTER #1. "Good!"

UGLY SISTER #2. "Kind!"

DIRECTOR. [*shouting*] That's enough! Learn the lines! That's it for the day.

Scene 5

[*Late evening. The* GIRLS' *dormitory. Eight beds, bedside tables, barred windows. The* GIRLS *are sitting up in bed (or lying down). One* GIRL *is asleep throughout. They are wearing uniform nightdresses with the reform school stamp.* CINDERELLA *is writing on a piece of paper.* STEPMOTHER *is preparing instruments for tattooing: she ties two needles to a pencil and mixes ink in an inkpot.*]

PRINCE. [*to* FATHER] You!

FATHER. What?

PRINCE. Look out.

FATHER. Again?

PRINCE. Look out!

STEPMOTHER. OK. Come here. [UGLY SISTER #2 *sits in front of her and opens her mouth.* FATHER *jumps out of bed, puts on slippers, and stands by the door, listening.* PRINCE *pulls out a pack of cigarettes from under her pillow.* STEPMOTHER *whistles.*]

FATHER. Jesus Christ, a smoke!

PRINCE. What do you think I was hanging around that electrician for?

STEPMOTHER. The director's all right.

PRINCE. Give me a break.

STEPMOTHER. He's got a BMW.

FAIRY GODMOTHER. A BMW? A BMW? Have you ever heard of a Mercedes? Christ! A BMW?

UGLY SISTER #2. [*to* STEPMOTHER, *ready with tattoo tools*] Come on, you ready?

STEPMOTHER. He'd be all right for a quick ride around the block. [*to* UGLY SISTER #2] OK. What do you want? R.I.C.H.? Remember I'll Come Home?

PRINCE. The director's a professional cocksucker. And he looks like a squealer.

STEPMOTHER. He can't help it if he looks like that. It's part of his job.

UGLY SISTER #2. No. B.I.T.C.H. Being Inside Turns Charity to Hate.

FAIRY GODMOTHER. [*ironically*] A BMW!

UGLY SISTER #2. It's one letter more, but I'll pay you.

STEPMOTHER. All right. Hold your lip out. [UGLY SISTER #2 *grips her lower lip between her fingers and pulls it out.* STEPMOTHER *starts to tattoo the inside of her lip very proficiently.*]

PRINCE. [*to* CINDERELLA] And what did the cocksucker want from you? Huh? Cinderella?

CINDERELLA. Nothing.

PRINCE. Sure.

CINDERELLA. Nothing, I said.

PRINCE. Why should you give a shit? Is it worth a smoke? [*pause*] Do you want a drag?

CINDERELLA. Nothing.

FATHER. [*from the door*] I'll take it. Give me one.

PRINCE. So we have smoke billowing out of the fucking keyhole into the hallway? No chance. Toe rag! [UGLY SISTER #1, *who has been lying silently on her bed, suddenly sits up, frightened*] Shoes! [UGLY SISTER #1 *leaps up, runs over to the* PRINCE, *takes her shoes, and starts polishing them with the sleeve of her nightgown.*] Use your hair! [UGLY SISTER #1, *without hesitating, spits on the shoes, and starts to polish them with her hair.*]

CINDERELLA. Give her a break.

PRINCE. She gets plenty of breaks. She's very happy. [*to* UGLY SISTER #1] Aren't you happy?

UGLY SISTER #1. Yes.

PRINCE. Well, could you be a little more cheerful about it? Come on, "I am very happy."

UGLY SISTER #1. I am very happy.

PRINCE. OK. Spit. [CINDERELLA *shrugs her shoulders and continues reading.*] How come you stand up for her? You feel sorry for a squealer?

FATHER. You smoked half my mattress. Just give me one drag. [PRINCE *throws her the cigarette stub.*] Tobacco. I don't believe it. [FATHER *drags on it so greedily, she burns her mouth.*]

PRINCE. Whose turn to tell a story?

FATHER. Mine.

PRINCE. Forget it. Who's next?

FAIRY GODMOTHER. Me.

PRINCE. Let's go.

MOUSE. [*whining to* STEPMOTHER] Hey, you promised to do a guitar on my back.

STEPMOTHER. Relax. I'll do it.

PRINCE. Get on with the fucking story.

FAIRY GODMOTHER. Well, she's on the run, and she meets up with this guy. They hit up this shop. They get away with leather jackets in three colors, pants that fit like this, cameras, watches, rings. Then they lose the stuff, get the cash, hit the road, drive to the beach.

PRINCE. And?

FAIRY GODMOTHER. They're in a hotel, sitting in the lounge, drinking coffee and booze. Then they go to bed.

PRINCE. Then what?

FAIRY GODMOTHER. Then they get busted. [GIRLS *react.*]

PRINCE. Screw that for a story. [*spits*] Toe rag! Wipe that up! [UGLY SISTER #1 *wipes it up with her nightie.*] With your hair. [*She wipes it up with her hair.*

PRINCE *looks at* CINDERELLA *for a long time.*] Cinderella!

CINDERELLA. What?

PRINCE. Bedtime with mother! [*pause*] Get on with it.

CINDERELLA. I did it yesterday.

PRINCE. I said bedtime with mother. We've been fucking around like stupid cunts with that movie all day—we need a break. I'll give you three cigarettes.

CINDERELLA. No.

PRINCE. Whatever you want. Tell us a story.

CINDERELLA. Lay off the toe rag.

PRINCE. Not on your life and a lot longer. [*pause*] Ask for something else. [*pause*]

UGLY SISTER #2. Ow! That hurts!

STEPMOTHER. Turn it out, or you'll smudge it! And blow on it. [UGLY SISTER #2 *blows on her turned-out lip.*]

PRINCE. I'll lay off her for three days. [CINDERELLA *says nothing.*] Four. [CINDERELLA *still says nothing.*] A week, and not a day more.

CINDERELLA. Swear to God?

PRINCE. Hope to die. OK? [UGLY SISTER #1 *bursts into tears.*] Oh, shut your mouth and get lost. [*to* CINDERELLA] Start talking.

CINDERELLA. OK. She's sixteen, with hair as yellow as flax.

PRINCE. As gold is better.

CINDERELLA. As gold. Her eyes are as blue as the sky. She's poor and ragged. She's got one pair of pants held up with a safety pin, and shoes that are all squashed. Her father's a drunk, her mother walks the streets, and her two older sisters treat her like shit.

PRINCE. Lazy cunts. Fucking whores.

CINDERELLA. Cars come and go. The sisters perm their hair and go out dancing with their boyfriends. One boyfriend manages a food store, the other's a stocktaker.

PRINCE. What's a stocktaker?

CINDERELLA. He counts the cans.

PRINCE. [*to* UGLY SISTER #2, *who is blowing her lip*] Stop snorting. Shut up, cunt. [UGLY SISTER #2 *tries to explain something—unintelligibly, since her lip is turned out.* PRINCE *throws a shoe at her. From now on, she dries her lip in silence.*]

CINDERELLA. All she has to sleep on is a couple of chairs. Until one day she goes to a coffee shop where there's a disco—

PRINCE. To a hotel!

CINDERELLA. To a hotel. Cabs keep pulling up, and elegant men with women like dolls get out. She's standing in the background getting pushed and shoved by everyone, and then she sees her sisters climbing out of a cab with their boyfriends. They point her out to each other and scream with laughter. And she just stands there, her blue eyes streaming with tears. Suddenly, with a squeal of brakes, a silver Mercedes sweeps up and stops.

MOUSE. Jesus!

PRINCE. With foreign plates?

STEPMOTHER. French!

PRINCE. No, American!

FAIRY GODMOTHER. Belgian!

PRINCE. Why Belgian?

FAIRY GODMOTHER. I don't know.

PRINCE. Fuck that!

CINDERELLA. A dark, handsome man gets out. He is slender as a willow; his hair is wavy—

PRINCE. Better if it's straight.

CINDERELLA. His dark hair is straight, and his eyes shine like a cat's. As he walks, the crowd pants. They stare at him. He's wearing a white suit, red bow tie, and a black shirt—

PRINCE. Stay-pressed. His shiny boots are gleaming . . .

CINDERELLA. Suddenly he stops, he's rooted to the spot—

FAIRY GODMOTHER. Oh, Jesus!

PRINCE. All the whores are trying to catch his eye.

CINDERELLA. All of them.

PRINCE. But he wouldn't even spit in their direction. [*She spits.*]

CINDERELLA. Wouldn't even spit. He just goes up to her, and speaks gently in a foreign language. She doesn't understand, but she can feel already that this is love. He takes her by the hand, on each finger he has a gold ring set with a diamond. He leads her to the door. She doesn't want to go. . . . She looks like shit, all in rags, but she follows. The bouncers let them pass; the waiters bow and scrape; he buys dinner for two—

FAIRY GODMOTHER. Oh, Jesus!

STEPMOTHER. How much?

CINDERELLA. Two hundred, each.

FAIRY GODMOTHER. [*together*] Jesus!

STEPMOTHER. [*together*] Two hundred!

CINDERELLA. They step out onto the dance floor. The

band bows; the bartender smiles. He waves his hand, and the band starts to play—

STEPMOTHER. A tango!

CINDERELLA. A tango.

PRINCE. What is it? "Strangers in the Night"? [*Starts humming the tune of "Strangers in the Night."* PRINCE *begins dancing, then other* GIRLS *and* CINDERELLA *join in. Some* GIRLS *clasp each other tightly as they dance.*]

CINDERELLA. All the lights go off in the club—there's just one pink spotlight on, and they're dancing right in the center. [*sings, inventing her own words*]
HERE WITH YOU TONIGHT
THE RAGS I'M WEARING:
HERE WITH YOU TONIGHT
THE PEOPLE STARING:
HERE ON SUCH A NIGHT
I FEEL MY DREAMS COME TRUE.
The sisters stand nearby, green with envy. But the couple goes on dancing; and everyone can see that this is love, and even though she's in rags, she's beautiful. And the boyfriends are furious that they didn't realize this before.

PRINCE. The pimps have tears in their eyes, and the whores sit with their mouths open . . .

CINDERELLA. And then, when it's almost morning, they leave. He takes her out for breakfast, and then they get married, and fly off to where he has a palace.

PRINCE. Of gold.

CINDERELLA. A palace of gold. And oil fields.

PRINCE. Kuwait.

FATHER. No, Texas.

FAIRY GODMOTHER. Mexico.

PRINCE. Why Mexico?

FAIRY GODMOTHER. I don't know.

PRINCE. Fuck Mexico!

STEPMOTHER. They've gotta come back.

MOUSE. Yeah, they've got to come back.

CINDERELLA. A year later she comes back with him, in a new Mercedes, gold-plated, covered with diamonds.

PRINCE. Forget it! That wouldn't last two minutes in the street! All the diamonds would be ripped off.

CINDERELLA. They're specially protected. You can't touch them or an alarm goes off.

PRINCE. Electronically and automatically.

CINDERELLA. Electronically and automatically. They arrive at her house and out she gets in a silver fox fur and stiletto heels. She's surrounded by a whole crowd of people, including her mother and father—both drunk—and her sisters. They're drunk too. And they look cold and hungry 'cause their boyfriends were put inside for having their fingers in the till. Everyone stares at her, but nobody recognizes her, until she says to her mother: "It's me, your daughter." Her mother and father fall on their knees and start to weep. They're afraid to go near her, 'cause they remember how they beat her and abused her. But she goes to them, and she forgives them. [The GIRLS *all have tears in their eyes. Some are crying out loud.*]

PRINCE. But not the sisters . . .

CINDERELLA. The sisters too.

PRINCE. Not on your fucking life and a lot longer. She can forgive the mother and father, OK. But not the sisters . . .

STEPMOTHER. What's it matter to you?

FAIRY GODMOTHER. Why can't she forgive them?

PRINCE. Fuck that!

CINDERELLA. Shall I go on?

PRINCE. Yeah, but without the sisters.

CINDERELLA. She takes her mother and father by the arm, and leads them over to the car—the back seat.

STEPMOTHER. They're gonna mess it up.

CINDERELLA. Then she goes up to the sisters. They're pissing in their pants.

PRINCE. Yeah!

CINDERELLA. But she gives them five hundred dollars each in one-hundred-dollar bills. They burst into tears and kiss her hands.

PRINCE. Now they're crying!

CINDERELLA. And she goes back to the car—

FATHER. [in a whisper] Look out! Deputy!

PRINCE. Quick! Get into bed! Lights out!

[PRINCE waves her arms in the air to get rid of the cigarette smoke. Lights go out. The only sounds are sniffing and muted crying. After a while, in the dim light, we see the door open. DEPUTY steps just into the dormitory with the DIRECTOR behind him. He stands in silence for a moment, then snaps his fingers twice. They both leave. Two GIRLS get up in silence and exit after them.]

ACT TWO   Scene 1

[*Rehearsal of the* PRINCE's *Ball. The* GIRLS *are trying on costumes. Some are fixing a painted clock to the wall: it's set at midnight.* PRINCIPAL *appears and greets the* DIRECTOR.]

PRINCIPAL. How's it going?

DIRECTOR. Well, we've having a few problems. Look, I'd like to tell you how sorry I am.

PRINCIPAL. Why? What's the matter?

DIRECTOR. Your wife's death. Very unpleasant.

PRINCIPAL. What are you talking about?

DIRECTOR. Poisoning herself—the post mortem—

PRINCIPAL. My wife is in excellent health. I just saw her an hour ago.

DIRECTOR. Are you sure?

PRINCIPAL. Of course.

DIRECTOR. Ah! Well, in that case . . . I'm sorry. I mean, I'm delighted! Congratulations!

PRINCIPAL. Thank you.

DIRECTOR. Stupid gossip.

PRINCIPAL. Think nothing of it.

[PRINCIPAL *strolls to the back of the stage and inspects the set preparations.* DEPUTY *enters.*]

DIRECTOR. Why did you give me all that crap about the Principal's wife?

DEPUTY. Apparently, I was misinformed. But supposing the Principal's wife is still alive?

DIRECTOR. There's no suppose about it. She is alive.

DEPUTY. That may be. In which case his aversion to women is all the more strange.

DIRECTOR. Does it matter?

DEPUTY. In theory, no. But, conversely—[*The* PRINCIPAL *approaches.*]

DIRECTOR. Principal, we are having a problem with Cinderella. She won't talk.

PRINCIPAL. Yes, so I heard.

DEPUTY. Perhaps we could encourage her.

PRINCIPAL. I don't understand.

DEPUTY. Apply a bit of pressure. Upset her a little.

DIRECTOR. She's playing the lead. Something has to be done.

PRINCIPAL. I can't help you there, I'm afraid. Are you familiar with the word "humanitarianism"?

DEPUTY. "Humanitarianism." What does "humanitarianism" mean to you? "Reading fairy tales I start to cry." Then they go home, and what happens? They run away from home straight back to this institution.

DIRECTOR. Are there such cases?

PRINCIPAL. Well, it has happened, yes.

DEPUTY. I'll tell you what "humanitarianism" is, shall I? It's humanitarian to give them a hard time—clap them into solitary on bread and water, shave their heads, cancel visiting time. Applying a little pressure. That's "humanitarianism."

PRINCIPAL. Well, I sometimes wonder about letting them get soft and then sending them back to their homes. But you're not talking about humanitari-

anism. You're talking about fireproofing. Are you
sure you're cut out for educating children?

DEPUTY. I completed the course with very high grades.

PRINCIPAL. I know that. But it doesn't alter the fact—

DEPUTY. To be quite candid with you, I was never all
that keen on this job. As a matter of fact, I was
going to be a pilot.

PRINCIPAL. A pilot?

DEPUTY. Yes.

PRINCIPAL. I had no idea.

DEPUTY. Yes. I wasn't doing too badly at all. But I always had trouble with taking off and landing.

PRINCIPAL. A considerable disadvantage.

DEPUTY. Do you know, I never managed a single landing?

PRINCIPAL. Then how on earth are you here?

DEPUTY. The instructors always took over.

PRINCIPAL. Why was it such a problem for you?

DEPUTY. I'm not sure. Anxiety, I think. I used to get
anxious because I was always the last to arrive for
roll call.

PRINCIPAL. Always the last? Why?

DEPUTY. Now that's an interesting point. Before I ran
out of the dormitory, I felt compelled to count the
beds.

PRINCIPAL. Why?

DEPUTY. I don't know. But since I had such a compul-
sion to do it, it must have been necessary, don't
you agree?

PRINCIPAL. I'm not sure. Perhaps.

DEPUTY. Absolutely. The trouble was, there were
eighty-two beds. If there hadn't been so many, I
wouldn't have always been so late.

[CINDERELLA *enters.*]

DIRECTOR. OK, let's go to work. [*leaving*] Cinderella is free for a moment. [*The* DIRECTOR *and* DEPUTY *leave.* PRINCIPAL *calls* CINDERELLA *over.*]

PRINCIPAL. Don't you want to take part?

CINDERELLA. I am.

PRINCIPAL. But you don't want to tell us anything about yourself.

CINDERELLA. No. So they got you to soften me up.

PRINCIPAL. In a way. Don't you like fairy tales?

CINDERELLA. Sure. But I've been told so many fairy tales in my life—especially by my father. The magic wore off pretty soon. So what happens now?

PRINCIPAL. That depends on you.

CINDERELLA. Aren't you going to frighten me? Tell me I'm out of luck if I don't cooperate, something like that? What are you looking at?

PRINCIPAL. I'm just looking.

CINDERELLA. Just don't pity me, for God's sake.

PRINCIPAL. If I pity anyone it's myself.

CINDERELLA. You?

PRINCIPAL. I have a few reasons.

CINDERELLA. Are you kidding? And I thought once you got to the top your worries are over.

PRINCIPAL. Why did you strike your stepfather? I think I know anyhow.

CINDERELLA. [*ironically*] I'm sure you read the trial reports. Don't tell me you've got any doubts? It was because I was jealous of my mother. My mother loved me so much and I got spoiled. When I realized she'd got a man—you know—I was seized with a dreadful despair that he would deprive me of her love. So, of course, I decided to kill him. I mean, it's understandable, isn't it? You would have acted the same in my place.

PRINCIPAL. I believe you were defending yourself against him.

CINDERELLA. And you can't see why I bothered. [PRINCIPAL *pauses.*] What's the difference? It's true that I shouldn't undermine my stepfather's authority, right? Discipline begins at home.

PRINCIPAL. And the shoes?

CINDERELLA. Oh, those. Mommy lent them to me.

PRINCIPAL. She testified otherwise.

CINDERELLA. She's got a short memory. She's not as young as she used to be.

PRINCIPAL. I saw your stepfather. He's very handsome. Must be about twenty years younger than your mother.

CINDERELLA. So what? Surely you know that age doesn't count when you're in love. And her money didn't exactly put him off.

PRINCIPAL. I see.

CINDERELLA. I doubt it.

PRINCIPAL. You don't want to talk about it.

CINDERELLA. It's not very interesting. He swore to her that he loved her so much he was prepared to adopt me. He told me he loved me so much he was prepared to marry my mother just to be close to me. It must have been true. He did marry her. Funny, huh? Why aren't you laughing?

PRINCIPAL. I'll start to in a minute.

CINDERELLA. Just imagine: you're a father, you're dying, and your wife—come to think of it, have you got a wife?

PRINCIPAL. Yes, why?

CINDERELLA. I'm only asking. Why?

PRINCIPAL. Nothing. Why?

CINDERELLA. Is something wrong? I wouldn't know.

PRINCIPAL. What are you talking about?

CINDERELLA. What a shame. You're all right really. Got problems with your wife, huh?

PRINCIPAL. Oh, you know . . .

CINDERELLA. Come on. Is she giving you a hard time? Getting it on the side? Or don't you love her anymore?

PRINCIPAL. What makes you think that?

CINDERELLA. I don't know. It happens. Well, what is it?

PRINCIPAL. There's really nothing to be said. An old friend of mine stopped by last week . . .

CINDERELLA. I understand.

PRINCIPAL. You understand what? It's not like that at all. But we had just been quarreling. She's fed up with me working here. I'm not getting promoted. The apartment's small, the TV's only black and white.

CINDERELLA. The usual. So what happened?

PRINCIPAL. Nothing. [*pause*] He stayed.

CINDERELLA. In what sense?

PRINCIPAL. Well, his name is Jan. You know the type —plays a lot of sports, goes to see French films.

CINDERELLA. What about him?

PRINCIPAL. She kept smiling at him, made a big deal over him. And I thought, I'm not going to put up with this much longer; so I didn't.

CINDERELLA. Did you let him have a piece of your mind? Or did you just let him have it?

PRINCIPAL. I went out for a walk. And she asked him to stay with her for good.

CINDERELLA. For good?

PRINCIPAL. For good.

CINDERELLA. And what about you?

PRINCIPAL. He asked the same question, and she replied: "This man is dead."

CINDERELLA. Fucking cow.

PRINCIPAL. He started to lay down conditions. He said he'd stay for a trial period—no more than a week. He told her she'd have to lose weight, and get up at six every morning to go jogging with him. If not, he'd leave, he said; and he asked me to witness the arrangement.

CINDERELLA. So what did you say?

PRINCIPAL. So I said, "As far as I'm concerned . . ." [pause] That's all I could say.

CINDERELLA. "As far as I'm concerned."

PRINCIPAL. What could I do? I gathered a few of my things together, and she said to me, "Fuck off, and quick." I said, "I am fucking off!" And he behaved quite decently.

CINDERELLA. Jan?

PRINCIPAL. Yes, Jan. "We're both Poles," he said. "We know the score. You can't say 'Fuck off' to someone you've lived with for seven years. 'Fuck off' is something you say to someone who provokes you on the street. 'Fuck off or I'll kill you.' And then if they don't fuck off he kills them."

CINDERELLA. A lot of laughs, your friend.

PRINCIPAL. He behaved like a gentleman. He even took me aside and asked me if I minded all that much. Said after all we were old pals, and he didn't want us to fall out all because of a woman.

CINDERELLA. Have you got a cigarette?

PRINCIPAL. What was I supposed to do? Plead with him? Plead with her? I don't smoke. I suppose you think . . .

CINDERELLA. I don't think anything.

PRINCIPAL. I wouldn't give you one anyway. That night I stayed at my mother's. Do yourself a favor. Stop smoking.

CINDERELLA. My stepfather gave me the same advice.

PRINCIPAL. [*with a happy smile*] That guy, Jan? We called him numb-nuts at school.

CINDERELLA. Numb-nuts?

PRINCIPAL. Numb-nuts.

CINDERELLA. Why?

PRINCIPAL. [*blue again*] I don't remember. [*A moment's silence.*]

CINDERELLA. How did you get along with her the rest of the time?

PRINCIPAL. Oh, not too badly. She had it in for me over the television, though. Being only black and white.

CINDERELLA. I don't mean that. I mean in general. How was it in bed? Did she shout at all? Or maybe she cried instead?

PRINCIPAL. No. But she did have tears in her eyes once.

CINDERELLA. That's a good sign.

PRINCIPAL. It is?

CINDERELLA. Any idiot can shout. But tears—that's a real performance.

PRINCIPAL. [*after a moment's silence*] Well, that's how
    it is.

CINDERELLA. Well, it's not so bad. Go back to her.

PRINCIPAL. Oh no, no, I can't do that. I can't forgive
    her. Especially since I don't know how she'd react.
    And there's Jan.

CINDERELLA. Do you love her?

PRINCIPAL. She didn't even let me take Flopper.

CINDERELLA. Who?

PRINCIPAL. He's a little mutt. Mine. He sort of at-
    tached himself to me in the park one day. He's
    white, not very big, with a brown nose. He always
    brought me luck. Well, that is . . . never mind.

CINDERELLA. I told you, go back to her. She loves you.
    She's just doing the same old number. For God's
    sake, do I have to explain everything to you? She
    got in too deep, and then couldn't back out. She
    wants you to deal with it.

PRINCIPAL. And how am I supposed to deal with it?
    Beat him up? Beat her up? Beat them both up?

CINDERELLA. If you ask me, she's already got rid of him.

PRINCIPAL. Jan?

CINDERELLA. Jan. Look, he probably wasn't that crazy
    about her. And if that was all she really wanted, she
    could have arranged it on the side.

PRINCIPAL. Do you think so?

CINDERELLA. Sure. Go back to her.

PRINCIPAL. And will she agree?

CINDERELLA. That depends on how you play it. But if
    you ask me, she'll beg you to stay. But you've got
    to put on a good act: say you've come for the rest
    of your things.

PRINCIPAL. What if she just says, "Fine, take them"?

CINDERELLA. Don't panic. She won't. Tell her she was absolutely right. There was nothing left of your life together. You're grateful to her for her honesty, and it's all for the best in any case, 'cause you've just met a really wonderful young girl. Well, you know, crap like that. There's no way she'll let you go then. But if you break down and start begging her, forget it. Remember: you're supposed to forgive her, not the other way around.

PRINCIPAL. She won't believe me.

CINDERELLA. She will.

PRINCIPAL. Well, I don't know. Maybe I ought to wait a few days. Maybe she'll come to me. Wait a minute. Maybe I'll just write that down. How did you put it exactly? That there's nothing left of our life together, that I'm grateful—yes?

CINDERELLA. And about the girl you've met. And just go on like that for a while.

PRINCIPAL. I'm not cut out for this kind of thing.

CINDERELLA. Nobody is.

PRINCIPAL. Well, I'll give it a try. I'm sure Flopper misses me. That's the dog.

CINDERELLA. I know. The mutt. At the very worst, you'll have to go back to your mother's.

PRINCIPAL. But it's so uncomfortable at my mother's.

Scene 2

[*Rehearsal of the ball scene is in progress. "The Blue Danube" on the piano. Some* GIRLS *are dressed as ladies and courtiers.* PRINCE *is in a red cloak—a bedspread.* CINDERELLA *is in the paper dress given to her by the* FAIRY GODMOTHER. DIRECTOR *is setting up the scene. All crew assembled on the set.*

Piano plays. GIRLS *dance.*]

DIRECTOR. You're happy! Smile! Smile! Prince, on the throne! Enjoy it! Enjoy it more! [*The grotesque couples dance in a row.*] Cinderella, you're standing near the dancing couples. Now the Prince notices Cinderella. But you must see her, see her! [PRINCE *stares ludicrously.*] Yes, that's right now. Get up slowly . . . slowly, with dignity. You stride over— you are the Prince! You go up to Cinderella. You kiss her hand. You look into her eyes. Cinderella curtsies. Deeper, deeper! Yes, that's right. You dance. Now, careful! The clock strikes twelve. You tear yourself away and cry out. [CINDERELLA *cries out.*] You turn and flee down the line of dancing couples, and the camera will track in front of you. You lose your slipper, stop for a moment, and then run out. The Prince runs after you, through the line of dancers. He spots the slipper, picks it up, fascinated. Fascinated! And then he turns to speak, then Cinderella . . . OK, let's take it from the top. Prince, on your throne. Going for a take now. Everyone on their marks. Silence on the set. Lights! Cinderella is standing over here. Piano, on my cue. Roll camera.

CAMERAMAN. Rolling.

SOUNDMAN. Speed.

CAMERAMAN. Mark it, please.

CLAPPERGIRL. Fifty-two, take one.

DIRECTOR. Action.

[*The whole scene is played out. Then the* PRINCE, *slipper in hand, speaks.*]

PRINCE. I'm in here for what you might call itchy fingers. I got a job as a high-powered hairdressing assistant. The people who did me the most harm were the ones I worked with. When some cash disappeared one day, they framed me. Next I was on the run. Next I see a girl walking toward me with these boots on. I really took a fancy to them. So I said to her, "Jump out of those boots," and she didn't seem too eager, so I smacked her one. Next things went pretty easy for a while, and I had a little think. I had talent, no doubt about it. Next I met up with some of the boys—villains—and next I was in with them. Next we did a heist on this jeweler—he was geriatric, you know, over thirty. Next I began to specialize in deep pocket work. I became the pickpocket queen. I had it made, right? And that was the beginning of my downfall. Next, thank God, I landed inside. I'd like to finish school, go to the university, and settle a few old scores, like killing my sister, for instance, who squealed to the law. I figure someone like that's got no right to live. I'd like to run into someone like that in a dark alley and teach them a few things. By hand. [CINDERELLA *stands before the camera. Long pause.*]

DIRECTOR. [*enraged*] Cut. OK, let's take a break.

CAMERAMAN. Save the lights!

DIRECTOR. It worked better in rehearsal, and your hands weren't shaking like that.

PRINCE. I forgot about them.

DIRECTOR. And all of you look happier! It's supposed to be a happy occasion. You're at a ball! You're going to get a free dinner . . . Dismissed.

[*The* GIRLS *leave.* DEPUTY *enters, holding several pieces of paper.*]

DEPUTY. I've prepared my lines, but I only want to be seen from the waist up, as I'll be holding my script.

DIRECTOR. Don't worry about that.

DEPUTY. I thought maybe you could use this as the opening of the film.

DIRECTOR. Great idea.

DEPUTY. A few lines. Do you want to have a glance at them?

DIRECTOR. No, no. I trust you. Get yourself ready. By the way, what about her?

DEPUTY. You mean Cinderella?

DIRECTOR. I mean Cinderella.

DEPUTY. No further developments. I'm ready when you are. It's just that my script mustn't be seen.

DIRECTOR. We have to get her to open up. I don't know, there must be some way . . . could we spring something on her? Listen, what if you tell her she's going to be released . . . we film her reaction to that, and then tell her it's not true, and we film her reaction to that.

DEPUTY. No, that's not a good idea.

DIRECTOR. All right, what if we tell her there's been an accident at home—something about her mother . . .

DEPUTY. No, that's no good. You've got to work on her pride. We'll set her up with your watch. Come on, give me your watch. Just go on working like nothing's happened, and when I come in in a moment, don't look surprised. Just listen, you'll get the gist.

DIRECTOR. OK. We'll see. [*The* DEPUTY *exits.*] One
more rehearsal. Places please. The courtiers are
asking the ladies to dance. That's right. Good!
Now the Prince asks Cinderella, and you two start
to dance. Everyone dance! [DEPUTY *strides in.*]

DEPUTY. Fall in for assembly! On the double!

DIRECTOR. Hold it! What's going on? [*The* GIRLS *form
into a line.*]

DEPUTY. An incident has occurred. The director, who
is making a film on your behalf, for your benefit
and with our permission, has discovered his watch
is missing—a watch of foreign manufacture. This
watch will be found within the hour. If it is not
found, the usual measures will ensue. Dismissed.
[*approaches* DIRECTOR] Well? What do you think of
that?

DIRECTOR. Well, we'll see what happens.

DEPUTY. Oh! Shall I do my bit while we're waiting?

DIRECTOR. Great idea. All right, stand over here—
that's it. Prepare. Concentrate, rest your hands on
that—that's it, very good. [DEPUTY *strikes an af-
fected pose, fidgets with his hair, buttons up his jacket.*]

DEPUTY. Just one more thing. The script, you know?

DIRECTOR. OK, going for a take.

CAMERAMAN. Could I just have a word with you?

DIRECTOR. What is it?

CAMERAMAN. Are you serious about shooting him?

DIRECTOR. Yeah, without the film. Take it out.

CAMERAMAN. Got you. OK, stand by. We'll go for a
take. No rehearsal.

DIRECTOR. [*to* DEPUTY] Are you ready?

DEPUTY. Just a minute. [*looks at himself in the camera,*

which is close to his face; smoothes his hair] Ready when you are.

DIRECTOR. Hold it a moment. Look, we'll tape your lines here, OK? Is that OK? [*He tapes the script to the camera, just under the lens.*]

DEPUTY. [*nodding approval*] Clever.

DIRECTOR. Lights! Roll camera.

CAMERAMAN. Rolling.

SOUNDMAN. Speed.

CAMERAMAN. Mark it, please.

CLAPPERGIRL. Fifty-three, take one.

DIRECTOR. Action! [CAMERAMAN *circles the* DEPUTY, *so he has to turn as he speaks.*]

DEPUTY. Welcome, ladies and gentlemen. I am one of the teachers of this institution. In effect, the problems of education in this country, albeit they are not fully solved, are very close to an ultimate solution. Our schooling is, step by step, comprising of more and more disciplines. The qualified team of those who are devoted to the rigors of teaching is rapidly expanding. We all fully possess an understanding of the giant strides of progress which have been taken in our country in this and every field, for our general well-being, of course. Nevertheless, we must not close our eyes to certain questions which, although not entirely representative, may, nevertheless, however, occasionally crop up, here and there, under certain conditions and on certain occasions, in their most elementary form. The problems—and let us not shrink from the use of that word—although it's not strictly accurate, though there's some truth in it—are marginal.

[*Toward the end of the* DEPUTY'S *speech, the* FAIRY GOD-MOTHER *approaches the* DIRECTOR, *curtsies, and hands him his watch.*]

DIRECTOR. What's this?

FAIRY GODMOTHER. Your watch has been found.

DIRECTOR. What!

FAIRY GODMOTHER. It was sitting in the washroom. Probably when you were washing your hands, you—

DIRECTOR. What washroom? Oh, all right. Thank you.

DEPUTY. Our film will explore dark and troubled regions which for the most part no longer exist. Also, problems that have been finally solved—not simply finally, but definitely—or if I may go so far as to say, not so much finally and definitely as completely.

DIRECTOR. Cut.

DEPUTY. What's the matter? Something wrong?

CAMERAMAN. Save the lights.

DIRECTOR. Yes. The watch has been found.

DEPUTY. What?

FAIRY GODMOTHER. On the windowsill.

DEPUTY. Now, look here, you. You know perfectly well where that watch was. So come on, tell us where it was found, or you could earn yourself another sentence.

FAIRY GODMOTHER. [*Looks around uncertainly, but meets* PRINCE's *cold stare. She turns back to the* DEPUTY *and speaks quietly.*] It was lying on the windowsill.

DEPUTY. Why don't you tell us where it really was?

FAIRY GODMOTHER. On the windowsill. [*As* DEPUTY

violently gestures, FAIRY GODMOTHER *cowers as if expecting to be hit.*]

DEPUTY. I'll get you for this. God save you, child.

DIRECTOR. What's going to happen now?

DEPUTY. I'll be finished with the filming in a moment.

DIRECTOR. What do you suggest next?

DEPUTY. They're onto us. They searched the dormitory and found the watch under Cinderella's pillow. The Prince delegated the Fairy Godmother to bring it back. The Prince is the ringleader, and she's covering up for Cinderella. But I'm going to find a way—

DIRECTOR. Look, I don't care. Just come up with something. You're supposed to be the fucking expert.

DEPUTY. All right. There's one foolproof way.

DIRECTOR. I thought this was supposed to be foolproof.

DEPUTY. This will be one hundred percent. The other was about eighty percent. Well, seventy-five percent. They really don't like squealers.

DIRECTOR. So?

DEPUTY. We have to frame her. It's got to look as if Cinderella's been squealing on the other girls.

DIRECTOR. And how do you propose to do it?

DEPUTY. Don't worry. I'll fix it.

DIRECTOR. How?

DEPUTY. Well, it's a trade secret, but I'll tell you anyway. The real squealer in their dorm is the Mouse. She's where we get our information.

DIRECTOR. What information?

DEPUTY. Where they stash their cigarettes, their tattooing equipment, what they talk about, things like that. The Mouse slips us a quiet word. We send for Cinderella and make a big song and dance. We have a talk with her for a half hour or so. Then immediately we charge into the dorm and confiscate some of the stuff the Mouse told us about. We shave a few heads. Threaten to extend a few sentences. That sort of thing.

DIRECTOR. Yes, this sounds better than the watch business. That seemed somehow immoral.

DEPUTY. Absolutely. Cinderella! You're to report to the Principal. He wants a word with you.

[DEPUTY *escorts* CINDERELLA *off. The stage empties. In the dim light, we hear the* GIRLS *singing "I don't fancy sweets anyway . . . "*]

Scene 3

[DEPUTY *enters with the* PRINCE *behind him.* PRINCE *hangs back, but the* DEPUTY *waves a hand and clicks his fingers, beckoning her over to him.*]

DEPUTY. Why are you looking at me like that?

PRINCE. Like what?

DEPUTY. Sort of purposefully. As if you wanted to say something, but didn't know how.

PRINCE. Are you talking to me or the wall?

DEPUTY. Oh my dear girl, my dear girl. Everyone who's approached says "no" at first. But give it time and anything can happen. After all, people are only human. You've been getting caught a lot lately. Bad luck, huh?

PRINCE. Bad luck, yeh.

DEPUTY. Oh. [*He lights cigarette.*] Nothing to smoke, eh? We found your butts. Well, never mind. When you get out in two or three years' time, you'll be able to smoke till your lungs disintegrate. Of course Cinderella will be smoking away sooner than that.

PRINCE. I don't hold it against her.

DEPUTY. Who's saying you do? You should be as pleased as I am—as the whole school is. Well. That'll be all. Here. [*gives a cigarette*] Let's get on with class. [*He presses a bell.* GIRLS *run in.* DEPUTY *sits at the piano.*] For today's class we shall practice the song you have written together then. So, tell me what it is.

FATHER. "In a Silent Cell."

DEPUTY. What's that?

FATHER. "In a Silent Cell."

[CINDERELLA *passes* DEPUTY *a piece of paper with the words written on it.*]

DEPUTY. [*looking at it*] Aha. [*plays a few bars of the mournful melody*] All together then! [DEPUTY *begins to play, and the* GIRLS *sing.*]

GIRLS. IN A SILENT CELL SO GLOOMY
WHERE I NEVER SEE THE LIGHT
I SHED MY TEARS FOR WASTED YEARS
AND FEEL THE BARS AROUND ME
    TIGHT.

SO DEAREST MOTHER, COME TO ME:
DEAREST MOTHER, VISIT ME.
TELL ME OF THE WORLD OUTSIDE
FOR I MISS IT TERRIBLY.

MY LITTLE BROTHER ASKS OF HER:

MOTHER, WHERE'S MY SISTER DEAR?
SHE'S SERVING TIME IN PRISON, SON:
SHE WON'T BE BACK FOR MANY A
        YEAR.

WHEN I'M DEAD AND AM NO MORE,
WHEN I'VE FOUND ETERNITY,
MOTHER DEAREST, ON MY GRAVE
PLANT A BLOOD RED ROSE FOR ME.

DEPUTY. Well, what can I say! Except, yes! Definitely, yes! I like that song! There's something about it that's genuinely moving. Or, as you might say, really makes a lump in the throat. I'd even go so far as to say I like it very much. How does it go? [*hums*] "In a silent cell so gloomy, where I never see the light." Quite frankly, I want to congratulate you, officially and personally. I'd just like to make a few very minor suggestions. Maybe one could try something instead of "gloomy" to make this cell, well, you know—different. As for "silent," "silent" is fine. Actually I like "silent"—it creates a specific atmosphere. But just because it's a cell, why does it immediately have to be dark? That— forgive me, won't you, but I have to say this—that is a classic example of artistic laziness, a cliché from nineteenth-century literature. I agree that now and then, here and there, one may come across cells like that. But the vast majority of cells are bright, clean, and tidy. And I feel the idea is that the cell in your song should be—you know— as it were, typical. Because this kind of pessimism is really uncalled for. It simply stems from ignorance of our ever-improving prison system and—

not to mince words—of the tangible ameliorations in the standard of our cells. So I have an idea. How does it go again?

GIRLS. [*singing*] IN A SILENT CELL SO GLOOMY.

. . .

DEPUTY. [*sings*] IN A SILENT CELL SO CHEERY!

GIRLS. [*sing*] WHERE I NEVER SEE THE LIGHT

DEPUTY. No, no, no. [*sings*] WHERE I ALWAYS SEE
THE LIGHT . . . !

There we are. That's a definite improvement. What comes next?

GIRLS. [*sing*] I SHED MY TEARS.

DEPUTY. Uh huh . . .

GIRLS. [*sing*] FOR WASTED YEARS—

DEPUTY. Hold it! [*sings*] FOR FUTURE YEARS—
OK. I shed my fears for future years.

GIRLS. [*sing*] AND FEEL THE BARS AROUND ME
TIGHT.

DEPUTY. [*sings*] AND FEEL MY SPIRITS SOAR TO-
NIGHT.

Well, there we are! Shall we take it from the top? Cinderella, you don't have to sing if you don't feel like it. Sit down. Have a rest. [CINDERELLA *shakes her head.*] All right, if you want to sing, sing. Ready, everyone! One, two, three—[*He sings with the girls.*]

DEPUTY & GIRLS. IN A SILENT CELL SO CHEERY,
WHERE I ALWAYS SEE THE
LIGHT,
I SHED MY FEARS FOR FU-
TURE YEARS
AND FEEL MY SPIRITS SOAR
TONIGHT.

DEPUTY. Now, let's have it faster, more cheerful! It's
    far better like this, but it's just that it's still too sad!
    I'll give you this as an introduction . . . [*He plays a
    marching tune.*] And we all come in! Let's try clap-
    ping hands as well! OK! One, two, three.
DEPUTY & GIRLS. IN A SILENT CELL SO CHEERY,
                WHERE I ALWAYS SEE THE
                    LIGHT,
                I SHED MY FEARS FOR FU-
                    TURE YEARS
                AND FEEL MY SPIRITS SOAR
                    TONIGHT.

DEPUTY. And once more with everyone clapping! Ev-
    eryone smiling! And . . . [*He and the* GIRLS *sing it
    over again happily.*] Let's see your teeth! [*breaks in*]
    I'm just wondering about one other thing in this
    verse. Just a tiny detail, but is it really a good idea
    for all this to take place in a prison cell? How about
    somewhere else? What do you think? Well, have a
    think about it. Because the whole point is that the
    changes and corrections should come from you.

[DEPUTY *exits.* PRINCE *nods her head at* STEPMOTHER,
*who runs to the door and listens. She gives a small signal to
the* PRINCE. *Some of the* GIRLS *grab* CINDERELLA. *One of
them sits at the piano and starts to play "IN A SILENT
CELL." They overpower her and thrust a towel into her
mouth. They push her down on one of the tables and tear off
her dress. Two* GIRLS *sit on her arms; one holds her head
down. Others take turns hitting her as hard as they can
with wet, knotted towels. The action is prolonged and
deadly serious. We see the towels rising and falling, and
hear the blows, in the tradition of lynch scenes. Suddenly*

PRINCE *whistles and the* GIRLS *scatter, leaving* CINDER-
ELLA *lying on the table. Only she and* PRINCE, *who is sal-
vaging something smashed during the skirmish, remain
onstage. After a while* CINDERELLA *slides down onto the
floor and crawls under the table, groaning.*]

CINDERELLA. Prince. [PRINCE *takes no notice of her. She
walks past the table.* CINDERELLA *tries to grab her
dress.*]

PRINCE. Hands off!

CINDERELLA. For God's sake, you know what's going
on.

PRINCE. You're telling me.

CINDERELLA. You're too smart to be taken in by all
this.

PRINCE. I don't talk to squealers.

CINDERELLA. You know it's not me! You know they set
me up.

PRINCE. It's not you that's squealing?

CINDERELLA. No.

PRINCE. Of course it's not. Why the fuck should it be?
[CINDERELLA *groans.*] So what's the problem?

CINDERELLA. Do the others know?

PRINCE. Why should they?

CINDERELLA. Explain to them.

PRINCE. If you want them to know something, explain
it to them yourself.

CINDERELLA. You're in with the Deputy.

PRINCE. I don't give a shit about the Deputy. I'm in
with number one. I'm holding onto my life.

CINDERELLA. You call this a life?

PRINCE. It's a life. More than you've got. You've
stepped out of line. They're gonna break you.

CINDERELLA. Maybe not.

PRINCE. They already have. Look at you now—pleading with me. You don't exist.

CINDERELLA. Tell them. He'll drop it if he sees it's not working . . . [PRINCE *moves to go.*] Wait!

PRINCE. I've got one last word for you, then I'm going.

CINDERELLA. What's your last word?

PRINCE. You're finished. Because you asked for it. They want to make this shitty film—you don't want them to make it. OK. But I want to get out of here. Either I go along with them. Or I don't. If I don't, they're going to make sure I don't get out. So I go along with them, and they go along with me.

CINDERELLA. And if they don't let you out?

PRINCE. Why shouldn't they? I'm not the one causing trouble—you are. I'm just sorry it had to be you. You're all right; you tell a good story. But you don't aim high enough.

CINDERELLA. So you're going to climb to the top of the heap?

PRINCE. That's right. The very top.

CINDERELLA. Know what I think of you?

PRINCE. I don't talk to squealers. I don't listen to them either.

Scene 4

[*The ball scene. Everyone dancing. One of the* GIRLS *plays the piano (“The Blue Danube”).* PRINCE *and* CINDERELLA *appear among the dancing couples. They dance formally in the foreground.* CINDERELLA *has a black eye; she looks sad and haunted. The film crew stand by.* DIRECTOR *gives instructions.* DEPUTY *enters.*]

DEPUTY. All going well?

DIRECTOR. What?

DEPUTY. Oh! Look at that shiner. That's very promising! I'd say the set-up worked. Won't be long now before she has—what would they call it?—a breakdown?

DIRECTOR. And if she doesn't?

DEPUTY. Oh, she will. Very hard for her to stick it out. Squealers are given a pretty rough time.

DIRECTOR. She's very tough.

DEPUTY. I'm telling you it will be very hard for her to stick it out.

DIRECTOR. Suppose she does?

DEPUTY. Not a chance.

DIRECTOR. But just suppose.

DEPUTY. It could only get worse.

DIRECTOR. It's not just me, you know. I can't go over schedule. I simply can't wait any longer.

DEPUTY. It won't be long.

DIRECTOR. We're spending public money—yours, mine, theirs.

DEPUTY. You could help a little yourself, you know. Tell her she's not doing it properly, can't act, moves badly—something along those lines.

DIRECTOR. But she's good.

DEPUTY. Well, thank God for that. That'd be all we needed—if after all this she couldn't even act. You should confuse her. When she's no good, praise her. When she's brilliant, criticize her. Do you see what I mean?

DIRECTOR. I suppose so.

DEPUTY. You won't be sorry.

DIRECTOR. [*resuming work*] Cinderella! No. Wrong.

All wrong. You look as if you've never danced in your life. What is that supposed to be, for Christ's sake? We'll take the whole thing again from the top. We'll all have to do it again because of you. All right, we'll go again. From the top.

[PRINCIPAL *enters and approaches* CINDERELLA.]

CINDERELLA. [*with venom*] What do you want?
PRINCIPAL. I wanted to thank you—it's going fine. With my wife, you know. Well, it was just as you said. You were right. She burst into tears.
CINDERELLA. Leave me alone. Are you finished, or what?
PRINCIPAL. Why have you got a black eye?
CINDERELLA. Oh, you've no idea, right?
PRINCIPAL. What are you talking about?
CINDERELLA. Forget it. [*She moves away.* PRINCIPAL *looks confused.*]

Scene 5

[*Dress rehearsal of the ball. The* DEPUTY *sits at the piano, playing "The Blue Danube."* DIRECTOR *picks on* CINDER-ELLA *a few times, making her repeat movements, carica-turing her. The* GIRLS *laugh. Finally, the* PRINCE, *while dancing with* CINDERELLA, *cuts the ribbons holding up her colored tissue paper skirt. The skirt falls and* CINDERELLA *stands in her underwear. The* GIRLS *and* ELECTRICIANS *burst out laughing.* GIRLS *press around* CINDERELLA, *shrieking with laughter, throwing her back and forth like a doll. They are vicious, relentless, their actions prolonged.* CINDERELLA *tries to shout above the* GIRLS. *She is unable to shout them down for some time.*]

CINDERELLA. Stop it, stop it! Stop it! Stop it! [*With a massive effort, she tries to break through the throng. The* GIRLS *don't give way immediately, their laughter unending. Finally* CINDERELLA *wrenches herself free.*] Well, is this what you want? You want a little circus, right? You want some fun? [*to* DIRECTOR] Is this what you want, or do you want something else? [*pulls out a razor blade*]

DIRECTOR. [*whispers to* CAMERAMAN] Full lights. We have to shoot this. [GIRLS *stand stock-still.*]

CINDERELLA. You want a big effect? I hope you're filming this in color! Here! [*slashes her hand with the razor*] Not enough for you? There. You like this fairy tale? You like this happy ending? You want more? [*slashes herself*] More? Well, how's that for you? All right? Or shall I go again from the top?

DEPUTY. Quite the little drama queen.

[*Silence except for the whir of the camera. One* GIRL *screams.* CINDERELLA *sways, wiping sweat from her forehead, and smearing blood all over her face.* PRINCIPAL *starts, as if from a dream, then runs toward her with a shout.*]

PRINCIPAL. Jesus Christ! Call a doctor!

[CAMERAMAN *focuses the camera on him.* PRINCIPAL *knocks it out of his hand.* CINDERELLA *stands amid the hubbub for a while, then sinks to the floor. The* DIRECTOR *grabs the fallen camera, picks it up, and continues filming.*]

BLACKOUT

[*After a moment, in darkness we hear the calm voice of one of the girls reciting the first line of the song that opened the play: "I'M FROM A RESPECTABLE HOME." Then another girl recites the next line: "I NEVER MEET BOYS ON THE QUIET." Two other girls recite together: "I NEVER GO OUT ON MY OWN," and finally still another girl finishes the stanza: "MY FOLKS WOULDN'T DARE LET ME TRY IT." Then all the girls begin to sing the second stanza without accompaniment: "I DON'T FANCY SWEETS ANYWAY, I WANT SOMEONE TO LOVE ME INSTEAD, WON'T SOMEBODY TAKE ME AWAY?" By the third line the singing becomes transformed into a desperate wail that sounds like a cry for help. The singing stops abruptly. The stage becomes brightly lighted. It's empty except for a pool of blood.*]

THE END

Hunting Cockroaches

CHARACTERS

Narrator
She
He
Immigration Officer
Czesio

Rysio (Nickname:
    Rysiu)
Bum
Mrs. Thompson
Mr. Thompson
Censor

The entire action of the play takes place in a Lower East Side Manhattan apartment.

ACT ONE

[*An elegantly dressed man appears in the spotlight on the forestage. He looks like a typical narrator in American films of a bygone era.*]

NARRATOR. [*smiles at the audience*] Good evening, ladies and gentlemen. In the early 1980s, during Ronald Reagan's administration, when the so-called Berlin Wall was still standing firm, wave after wave of Eastern European emigrants poured into the United States in quest of a better life and freedom. The greatest number of them came here from the country of Pulaski, Kosciuszko, and Lech Walesa. Our heroes have been chosen from among hundreds of thousands of ordinary people. Let us follow their first steps on American soil. The beginnings were far from easy, although . . .

[*The* NARRATOR *disappears. Then we see a squalid, shabby room serving as living room, bedroom, and kitchen. A door leading to the bathroom. A mildew spot in one corner of the ceiling. Two barred windows. Furniture placed haphazardly, piles of clothes here and there. An old wheelchair is clearly visible. Tea bags hang on a rope, drying. There are papers and dictionaries piled on a table by the window. Several small replicas of the Statue of Liberty stand on a shelf. A huge map of America hangs on the wall.*
In the middle of the room there is a large bed. A single

*bare light bulb hangs directly above the bed. The light can
be switched on and off by pulling a cord.* HE *is in the bed,
asleep, unseen by the audience, with a blanket pulled over
his head. Suddenly the bathroom door swings open and* SHE
comes out with her back toward the audience. SHE *is wearing a nightgown, with a kitchen towel on her arm and a
used tea bag in her hand. Slowly and dramatically* SHE
starts to recite parts of Lady Macbeth's soliloquy. SHE *seems
to be addressing the absent Macbeth as though he were hidden in the bathtub behind the plastic curtain.*]

SHE. [*recites from Macbeth and looks at her hands*] Yet
here's a spot . . . Out damned spot! Out, I say!—
One; Two; Why then 'tis time to do 't!—Hell is
murky!—Fie, my lord, fie! A soldier, and afeard!
. . . What, will these hands ne'er be clean?—No
more o' that, my lord, no more o' that; you mar all
this with starting . . . Here's the smell of the
blood still: all the perfumes of Arabia will not
sweeten this little hand. Oh! Oh! Oh! . . . Wash
your hands, put on your nightgown; look not so
pale:—I tell yet again, Banquo's buried; he cannot
come out of the grave . . . To bed, to bed: there's
knocking at the gate. Come, come, come, come,
give me your hand. What's done cannot be un-
done: To bed, to bed, to bed.

[*While delivering the soliloquy* SHE *tidies up the room;
hangs the used tea bag alongside several other ones on the
rope above refrigerator, then climbs up on the edge of the
bathtub and hangs the kitchen towel on the curtain rod. By
the end of the soliloquy for the first time* SHE *turns around
and seems to be taken aback by discovering the audience. A
fleeting smile, half-embarrassed, half-coquettish, flashes*

across her face, and in an instant SHE *hops into the bed, and again gives the audience a look that asks for their support.*]

HE. [*still invisible from under the covers*] Turn off the light.

SHE. [*with an impatient gesture of her hand, orders* HE *to keep quiet, gets up out of bed, and addresses the audience.*] My name is Anka. I can't sleep. I'm a nervous wreck. I'm Polish. I've been in New York for three years. For the past three months I can't get any sleep. I mean, at first I couldn't sleep for something like a month, then I could, and then I couldn't and then I could again. Now for the past forty-two days—or maybe it's twenty-two days—I can't sleep at all. [*studying the audience*] I'm an actress . . . I can't get any parts due to my accent. They say I have an awful accent . . . do I? That's my husband, Janek . . . [*points to him*] He can't sleep either. He's just pretending he's asleep. . . . [*smiles*] I know it. He can't fall asleep without his pills and I hid them. [*looks around, pulls a bottle of pills from under the mattress, and shows them to audience*] See! [*smiles triumphantly*] To tell the truth the pills don't help him any, he loves searching for them. He's a writer . . . He was very famous in Poland. . . . a novel of his came out in Paris . . . One of his plays was produced in New York. [*looks around the audience*] His name is Krupinski, Jan Krupinski. [*pauses for a moment. . . . spelling*] K R U P I N S K I. . . . Never heard of him? It's a good thing he's asleep. I mean, he's pretending . . . Look, I've got a whole bunch of reviews. He got a very good one in the *New York Times,* and a real bad one in the *Village Voice.* I got an award for my interpretation of Lady Macbeth in Warsaw. I know it's completely moronic, but here in America you have to praise yourself, right? If you don't have any confidence in yourself, who's going to? Do I really have an awful accent? I did some work for an art critic from Poland who's well connected. He works in an Italian restaurant at Second Avenue and Eighty-eighth Street. He got me a temporary job at the Museum of Immigration. I'd appear every noon dressed as a nineteenth-century Polish emigrant. You know the outfit . . . babushka, boots [*ironically*]. But now the museum is being repaired. . . . [*throws up her hands as if to say, "What can I do?"*] Isn't he good at pretending he's asleep. I taught him how. If it gets out he can't sleep, we're finished. In New York everybody knows how to sleep. I'm trying to get him to pretend he's happy. In New York everybody's happy. [HE *groans.*] In the daytime he usually sits in front of the map. [SHE *points to the map hanging on the wall.* SHE *gets up and goes over to the map, sits down in front of it, looks at the map for a while in silence.*] He can sit like this for an hour or two. [*Again* SHE *looks at the map in silence.*] Then he says: "What a strange country!" That's all. "What a strange country!" I told him he'd never make it here because he doesn't have a sincere smile. Everybody here has a sincere smile. And he's got a nasty one. He took it very hard. In eastern Europe nobody has a sincere smile, except drunks and informers. [*smiles*] Yesterday he sat in front of the map and practiced the art of the sincere smile, checking it every so often in the mirror. I told him he should write a play about Polish émigrés, but he said the subject is boring, either you make it or you don't.

HE. [*waking or pretending to wake up*] What time is it?

SHE. [*rapidly walks to the window, looks out into the street at the large clock on the corner.*] One hour later than usual. Lately you are asking me what time it is at three in the morning—now it's four in the morning.

HE. You are screaming again . . . Lately you scream in your sleep all the time.

SHE. Do I?

HE. You sit up in the bed and scream. [*imitates her scream*]

SHE. You'll wake up everybody in the building.

HE. Then you go back to sleep immediately.

SHE. Immediately.

HE. Immediately. But then I can't fall asleep.

SHE. Yes, I know, in the morning you have your lecture at Staten Island Community College. Where they pay you nothing, but help us with our application for the green card. And you hate your classes, because: "How can you teach Franz Kafka to students who drive to school in sports cars?" . . . All right, let's go to sleep. [HE *turns light out. They pull the blanket over their heads. Moment of silence.*] Oh my God! [SHE *turns light on.*]

HE. What are you dreaming about?

SHE. I'm not dreaming about anything.

HE. You weren't dreaming about anything?

SHE. No. I wasn't even asleep.

HE. But why do you start screaming?

SHE. Because I felt like it.

HE. Maybe you were dreaming that we were back in Poland.

SHE. No.

HE. Or that somebody broke into the apartment through the window.

SHE. We have heavy iron bars on all the windows. No one can get through those bars.

HE. No harm checking. [*at the window, shakes the bars*] No, with those bars there, it would be impossible for anyone to get through that window. Your dreams are absolutely moronic.

SHE. [*a look of disgust on her face, whacks the floor hard with her shoe, then whacks it again*] It ran under the floorboard.

HE. Cut it out. That old bag under us will call the super. He's been waiting for a chance to get rid of us. Do you know how much he'd get for an apartment like this? Nowadays, in a neighborhood like this? On the Lower East Side?

SHE. Oh, it's a terrific neighborhood all right. Some apartment. Constantly broken into, fifth floor without an elevator, cold in winter, hot in summer, and you can't put an air conditioner in because the fuses will be blown . . .

HE. We can't afford an air conditioner.

SHE. Muggers, rapers . . .

HE. It's a neighborhood for artists.

SHE. For cockroaches.

HE. What do you have against cockroaches? New York is full of cockroaches. They're everywhere. Even in millionaires' houses.

SHE. How do you know? Have you ever been in a millionaire's house?

HE. Cockroaches don't spread infection, and they eat only garbage. Remember Gregor?

SHE. Gregor who?

HE. The hero of Kafka's *Metamorphosis*. The one who was transformed into a cockroach. His sister used to bring him fresh rolls, cheese and milk . . . he wouldn't even spit on it. The only thing he'd touch was garbage.

SHE. I've seen them touch our caviar.

HE. Even if they did, how much food could a cockroach eat?

SHE. Then it's the rats who eat up our food.

HE. The mice.

SHE. The rats.

HE. They're big mice. Anyhow, the mice eat the cockroaches.

SHE. How do you know?

HE. I watched them.

SHE. I heard that rats eat children.

HE. We don't have any children.

SHE. Aha. . . .

HE. For God's sake, don't start that about having a baby. That's all we'd need. A baby. I want to know where we'd put it?

SHE. Over there. [*points*]

HE. And what about us?

SHE. Over here.

HE. And what about me? Where'd I do my writing?

SHE. You're not doing any writing.

HE. I have nothing to write about.

SHE. Have you ever thought about writing nursery rhymes?

HE. Enough about a baby.

SHE. That would change everything. You'd start writing. You wouldn't have any other way out.

HE. I'd always have one way out. Through the window.

SHE. With those iron bars?

HE. Let's go to sleep.

SHE. Let's. [*Humming a lullaby, "Aa, kotki dwa, szare, bure obydwa . . . " (Aa, pussycats two, both of them are black, both of them are blue . . .) with the heavy movements of a woman in the last stages of pregnancy,* SHE *climbs into bed and turns light out. The phone rings and wakes them up. With a start they both jump out of bed. In the process the pillow slips out from under her nightgown.*]

HE. What time it is?

SHE. Ten past four.

HE. Who could be calling at this time of night? [HE *turns light on.*]

SHE. I have no idea.

HE. Burglars? Maybe they're checking to see if we're in? [*The phone keeps ringing.*]

SHE. Well, answer it if you're so curious.

HE. Maybe it's the super. I told you not to pound on the floor. Maybe it's . . . [*starts to whistle*]

SHE. Stop that whistling. [HE *keeps on whistling.*] You always whistle when you're afraid of something. I can't stand it any longer. Maybe it's who?

HE. KGB?

SHE. KGB?

HE. To scare me.

SHE. But why would they want to scare you?

HE. Because they know I hate them. Because I'm a writer, an émigré writer, and I could write something.

SHE. But you're not writing anything.

HE. But I could start writing at any time.

SHE. Then start.

HE. But I don't have anything to write about.

SHE. Why would they want to scare you? You're already scared of them. Maybe it's the Immigration Office.

HE. What for?

SHE. I don't know. Maybe someone squealed on us.

HE. Squealed about what?

SHE. That our visas expired.

HE. But they promised we'd get green cards.

SHE. But we didn't get them yet. We've still got to go for another interrogation.

HE. It's not an interrogation, it's an interview. The fact that we got the notice to go means that everything's fine. Millions of people in New York are just waiting for that.

SHE. To go for an interrogation?

HE. To go for an interview. [*The phone keeps ringing.*]

SHE. Maybe someone's calling from Europe? The time's different there. What time it is in Europe now?

HE. What time it is here?

SHE. Quarter past four.

HE. Then in Europe it must be . . .

SHE. In the morning?

HE. Yes.

SHE. Then it has to be someone from Europe.

HE.   Andrzej is in France. Maybe he's calling. But just what do you think he wants from us? Oh, I know, of course. He is jealous.

SHE.   Jealous? Of what?

HE.   What do you mean of what? He emigrated only to Paris, and I am in New York, and I made it here.

SHE.   But you didn't make it.

HE.   But he doesn't know it. Maybe we should answer the phone.

SHE.   Maybe we should. [*Bending over the telephone, they wordlessly encourage each other to pick up the receiver. Just at the moment* HE *reaches for it, the phone stops ringing.*]

HE.   Damn it, why did you tell me not to answer it? Now it's too late. [*The phone starts to ring again, twice only.*]

[*A typical immigration* OFFICER *crawls from under the bed. He spreads his papers and leafs through them. He's a very nice little bureaucrat and smiles radiantly throughout the interview.*]

OFFICER.   Would you come over here. Both of you, please. [*The immigration* OFFICER *takes their finger-prints, looks at Jan's legs.*] What's wrong with your leg? Aren't you limping a bit?

HE.   No, I'm not. My leg just fell asleep.

OFFICER.   Aha . . . Now your turn, lady. Thank you. That's all.

HE.   Immigration asks everyone the same questions.

SHE.   Absolutely everyone?

OFFICER.   [*to* HER] Do you intend to engage in prostitu-tion while you're in the United States?

HE.   Take it as a compliment.

OFFICER. You haven't answered my question yet.

SHE. No, of course not, I don't intend to. But if I may . . .

OFFICER. Thank you. [*to him*] Did you come to America with the intention of killing the President of the United States? [HE *clears his throat.*]

SHE. Is that a standard question?

OFFICER. I'm waiting for your answer.

HE. No. To tell the truth . . . I don't understand.

OFFICER. Thank you. [*puts his papers away*] No more questions. That's all we wanted to know. [*takes a step toward the bed, then stops*] One more question. Have you ever been treated for VD?

SHE. What kind of VD?

OFFICER. That's exactly what I'm asking you.

SHE. No, never.

OFFICER. [*to him*] And you?

HE. No, never.

OFFICER. Thank you. You'll be notified when to appear for the next interview.

HE. Spytaj o pieniądze.

SHE. Excuse me, sir.

OFFICER. Yes?

SHE. Is it possible to obtain a temporary work permit? You see, we're in some financial difficulties, nothing serious but . . .

OFFICER. Sorry, that's impossible. But I don't want you to worry. As long as you don't work without a permit, you can sleep in peace.

HE. Thank you very much.

SHE. Thank you very much.

OFFICER. Not at all. Good luck to you. [OFFICER *starts folding papers, disappears under bed.*]

HE AND SHE. Good luck to you.

SHE. What I'd really like to know is whether they think
that if you'd come to kill the President you'd give
them an honest answer. [SHE *turns light out.*] Is
crabs a venereal disease?

HE. You never mentioned to me that you had crabs.

SHE. Oh, I am mentioning it now to keep the conversation going. [HE *turns light on.*]

HE. Interesting. I have no idea whether crabs is a venereal disease or not. I never gave it much thought.
[*Phone rings three times.*] In Poland once I met a
guy who'd spent five years in prison, and I wanted
you to know he told me he was really glad to have a
rat in his cell. They became friends.

SHE. You told me the same story before, but last time
the guy was really glad to have a spider in his cell.

HE. I'm sure I said it was a rat, the spider was in a Du-
mas book. *The Count of Monte Cristo, Part II.*
[*Roach crawls across bed.* HE *whacks it away and
stomps on floor to scare it.*] That cockroach was the
size of a sparrow.

SHE. Get it.

HE. It got away—into the cracks in the floor. It ran
into the cracks because that's where they do their
hatching. They hunt at night and hatch eggs during the day. It's interesting, cockroaches don't like
coffee. [*From the floor below comes the sound of
pounding on the ceiling with a broom.*] Oh God, how
I hate that old hag. She gets excited at the slightest
sound. Why doesn't she go to sleep? When I saw
that old hag for the first time, and she threatened
to call the police, I understood for the first time
that in Dostoyevsky's *Crime and Punishment* it's

not just a theoretical problem about whether killing one's fellow man is ever justified and under
what circumstances. I bet Dostoyevsky lived in a
building in St. Petersburg with an old hag like that
directly underneath him, and that's how he got the
idea. Cockroaches are fast learners. There's no
doubt about it. It's strange that there aren't any
cockroaches in Poland. Maybe they locked them
up somewhere? Or maybe they sent all the cockroaches off to take an indoctrination course? The
older ones are much more cunning. The younger
ones don't run for cover if you turn the light on.
See! [*demonstrates*] I'm talking about the littlest
ones.

SHE. The babies.

HE. All the older, smarter ones run straight under the
boards. I wonder why cockroaches don't like coffee. [*mounting sound of a siren*]

SHE. That's the same one as yesterday. Recognize it?
Now here's where it gets stuck. There, it's just the
same as yesterday.

HE. All the sirens sound the same.

SHE. That's the one we heard yesterday. Do you hear
that? Now it goes way down in the lower register.

HE. You're talking nonsense. Let's go to sleep.

SHE. I'm telling you. That siren has a personality all its
own. It's trying something fancy. Usually it goes
"uuuuu" not with this "buuuum." Maybe he's
trying to give us a clue about something.

HE. That there's a fire somewhere. Listen, will you, I
have to get up early for my lecture.

SHE. I know. You have to lecture about Franz Kafka to
girls who drive to school in Mitsubishis. Kafka

would have a good laugh. You simply envy them their Mitsubishis.

HE. I won't fall asleep. [HE *switches off light.*] I know I won't be able to fall asleep. [*A moment of silence. Then suddenly* SHE *says* . . .]

SHE. Milk!

HE. Oh no! [SHE *turns on light.*]

SHE. Milk is good for sleeping. Cold milk.

HE. What are you talking about?

SHE. I meant to say hot milk. Hot milk helps you get to sleep.

HE. I hate milk. Especially hot milk. I love cold milk. You look awful. Actually you look green.

SHE. I can't sleep.

HE. Neither can I.

SHE. I know. You look like a corpse.

HE. Like a corpse?

SHE. That's right. I'm sure hot milk would do us both a lot of good.

HE. Didn't we already try hot milk?

SHE. Yes. [HE *turns light out. They put the blanket over their heads. They lie in silence for a couple of moments.*]

SHE. I didn't think you'd ever have the nerve to go up there.

HE. I got on the elevator. I got off at the nineteenth floor. They're on several floors.

SHE. I didn't know that.

HE. The nineteenth, the twenty-first, and the twenty-third.

SHE. Three whole floors? [SHE *turns light on.*]

HE. Three whole floors!

SHE. I hope you got there just before noon.

HE. Why?

SHE. That's the best time to go see Americans. Just before lunchtime when they're about to get something to eat.

HE. Here in America nobody asks what you had for lunch, but who you had lunch with. That's why I got there at two.

SHE. Aha.

HE. There's a dirty old corridor. On the right, behind a glass window there's a receptionist acting as a guard. Just like at police headquarters. [*laughs*] A blonde. Not half bad.

SHE. Was she young?

HE. Very.

SHE. Wearing glasses?

HE. Why do you ask?

SHE. I just thought she might be wearing glasses.

HE. No, she wasn't wearing glasses. I thought the office of such an influential magazine would look quite different.

SHE. Like what?

HE. I thought there'd be antiques, old china, flowers, Chagall's paintings, everything in good taste. But their walls look just like our walls. I went over to her.

SHE. Over to whom?

HE. To the guard. The blonde. I smiled.

SHE. [*frowning*] You didn't have to do that.

HE. [*irritated*] That's where you're wrong. She liked my smile. She smiled back. Not everyone thinks the way you do. [HE *flashes a prolonged and sincere smile. Then the smile fades away.*]

SHE. Well, well. . . .

HE. So I said that I'd like to see the editor.

SHE. Aha.

HE. Then she looked me over carefully.

SHE. She looked you over carefully?

HE. Very carefully. And she said she was sorry but that it was impossible . . .

SHE. Impossible.

HE. Then I told her everything about myself. And she smiled again.

SHE. Did she call the editor?

HE. No. She went out for a little bit. Then she came back and said the editor would see me immediately.

SHE. Immediately?

HE. That's right, see me immediately. You can imagine how I felt.

SHE. Yes. And what happened?

HE. The editor saw me.

SHE. The editor himself?

HE. The editor himself.

SHE. What was his name?

HE. I don't remember.

SHE. Didn't he give you his card?

HE. He doesn't have to have a card. Does Reagan need a card?

SHE. No, he doesn't need a card.

HE. Or does the Pope?

SHE. Personally, I deeply admire the Pope. Unfortunately he is a little bit too religious.

HE. I introduced myself. He asked me to sit down and he told me he's very interested in me, Poland, Solidarity, and Lech Walesa.

SHE. Did he give you a cup of coffee?

HE. Yes, and I gave him my story.

SHE. Did he take it?

HE. Of course. He said he was glad to have it, and that I should call him in two weeks.

SHE. In two weeks?

HE. That's a very short time. You have no idea how long it usually takes. Then I apologized. For taking up his time like that.

SHE. What did he say?

HE. He just laughed . . . But it was a quick laugh. [*demonstrates how*]

SHE. That's quick. But don't worry. All Americans in responsible positions laugh quickly so as not to waste time. He must have liked you.

HE. [*smiles happily*] You know, I think he did.

SHE. That's great. Once we get money we'll move uptown. To Fourth Street. It's much safer there. The floors are thicker, you can smash cockroaches and they don't hear you downstairs.

HE. Don't get excited. [HE *turns light out.*]

SHE. I know perfectly well that you didn't go anywhere, that you chickened out and that you feel bad about it, that you think you're dumb, and that you hate yourself. You didn't see the editor, and I even suspect you didn't get as far as the elevator.

HE. [*turns light on*] Look at me. Do you see what I look like? [*sits on bed*] Do you see?

SHE. [*looks him over carefully*] Yes, I see.

HE. And?

SHE. And what?

HE. I mean, how could I have gone there in the state I'm in. You can see for yourself . . . You said it: I look like a very sick man.

SHE. Oh no, like a corpse. I said you look like a corpse.

HE. It's because I don't get enough sleep.

SHE. I know.

HE. I constantly bump into things, the buttons on my shirt come off, I spill my coffee, I can't go and have a drink with anyone because I'll spill it as soon as I try to take a sip. It isn't even that what I say is such nonsense, but I say it at the wrong times before I should or when it's too late; what I want to say would be just fine if I only knew the right moment to say it. Anyone who looks at me can see that I don't get enough sleep.

SHE. So what? I bet that Kafka didn't get enough sleep either, and actually the great German philosopher Max Scheler died from insomnia.

HE. Well, that's just why nobody would ever take them seriously here.

SHE. Have a glass of milk.

HE. I took an elevator to the seventeenth floor, I went over to the secretary, I looked at her, she looked at me, and it all became clear.

SHE. What?

HE. We're both insomniacs.

SHE. Don't bite your nails.

HE. That's exactly it, she bit her nails too. We looked at each other and we both bit our nails.

SHE. And then what happened?

HE. And then I noticed that she had a button missing on her blouse and she noticed that one of my pockets was torn. While she was trying to fix her blouse, she spilled her coffee. And I tried to hide my torn pocket, but then my manuscript went all over the floor. There wasn't a chance she'd let me get through.

SHE. Why not?

HE. Insomniacs have fear and contempt for other insomniacs. Only a sleeper can help me. Sound sleepers run New York, the problem is how to get to them. Insomniacs won't let you, they are very crafty. They pretend, and look well rested. They dress very carefully, they put makeup under their eyes. Only their movements give them away.

SHE. What movements?

HE. [*knocks an empty glass to the floor*] And they boast too much about what a good night's sleep they've had. No more than ten percent of all the people in New York sleep.

SHE. Why is that?

HE. Because of the émigrés coming here. What do you think of my theory?

SHE. I think you've gone crazy.

HE. Once I had a chance to get into the world of real sleepers. The Thompsons were ready to introduce me.

SHE. Don't start that again.

HE. You ruined all my chances. You behaved like a barbarian.

SHE. I know. I know it all by heart. I wonder how long you're going to keep pestering me about that? I really . . .

HE. I want you to know that I'm unable to sleep, that I pace back and forth in the room and [HE *demonstrates.*] that I bump into the wardrobe, there, you see! I'm not fit to live, and it's all thanks to you.

[HE *goes over to the wheelchair standing in the corner, slumps into it, and rolls to the front of the stage.*]

SHE.   What do you have to say about that?

HE.   And just what does that wheelchair have to do with it?

SHE.   If only you hadn't brought that wheelchair home . . . You came home very pleased with yourself that day. You'd met Tomek in a wheelchair going off to work. You asked him what was wrong with him, and he said there was nothing wrong with him, he just bought himself a wheelchair to avoid paying the rent. A landlord has no right to evict an invalid, that's right isn't it? And the next day you brought home that wheelchair.

HE.   It was in very good shape. I found it thrown out on the street as trash.

SHE.   You wanted me to pretend to be an invalid and spend the rest of my life in a wheelchair.

HE.   What makes you think that? That's absurd.

SHE.   Then why did you bring it home? Answer me that!

HE.   It's a nice comfortable wheelchair. In mint condition. It could be the pride of any home.

SHE.   Why did you say you were curious to find out whether I'd know how to use it? [*Furious,* SHE *grabs the back of the wheelchair and stops it from rolling.*]

HE.   Out of curiosity. Do you really think I'd make you spend the rest of your life in a wheelchair? Just to save three hundred fifty dollars a month?

SHE.   Of course, I do. You'd make me do it to save even five dollars a month. [SHE *pushes him into the bathroom, slamming the door.*]

HE. Three hundred fifty dollars is a lot of money. [HE *reappears from the bathroom.*]

SHE. Do you want to go back to Poland?

HE. I don't know.

SHE. We can't go back.

HE. I know. [*pause*] I'll go to the magazine. [*pause*] Tomorrow.

SHE. You won't ever go, so stop lying to yourself—and to me. You've always lied to me.

HE. No I haven't. Not in Poland.

SHE. Didn't you read me T. S. Eliot's *Waste Land* and say you wrote it?

HE. I wanted only the best for you. My poems weren't as good. I loved you.

SHE. Listen, there's one thing I want you to do for me. All the Polish émigrés here are going crazy. I implore you: don't lie. Or you'll start to believe your own lies. Like Krzysiek who believes he's making a movie, and Grazyna who's convinced she's working for CBS. You'll end up like that. You'll jump off the George Washington Bridge.

HE. Don't worry. To get there you need a car. [*The phone starts ringing again.* SHE *automatically picks up the receiver.*]

SHE. Hello, oh, it's you, Zosia. Zosia is calling from Queens. Yes, it's late, but this is New York, no? You're lucky you reached us. We went to the theater and then to eat Chinese as usual. Did we call you before? No? Did you call us? No reason, I'm really glad you called. What? Wlodek sold six paintings? That's wonderful, congratulations. [*pause*] A whole article in the *Times*? That's wonderful. I mean, he certainly deserves it. If you're good enough, you'll always make it. It takes talent and hard work. We? Jan was at the *New Yorker* today, the editor had heard about him, loves his work, he was really glad to meet Janek. For sure we didn't call you before. Are you sure you didn't call us? Have a nice day. It was great talking to you. Love to Wlodek from both of us. [SHE *finishes the conversation and puts the receiver down. They both sit in silence for a while.*]

HE. It's a strange country. [*The mounting sound of a fire siren.* SHE *grows animated.*]

SHE. There it goes again. A real artist. [SHE *turns out the light.*] What are we going to do?

HE. I don't know. [HE *begins looking for something.*]

SHE. What are you looking for?

HE. Sleeping pills.

SHE. I'll help you. [*They look together for a while.*]

HE. There were at least ten pills left in the bottle.

SHE. What happened to it?

HE. It was here by the bed.

SHE. Maybe in the bathroom?

HE. They were standing by the bed. [*They continue looking for the pills.* HE *pulls out things from the drawer of a nightstand.*] Look what I find here: your amber jewelry and a leatherbound edition of *Faust.* You were going to sell them when we first got here, and the caviar too.

SHE. I was going to sell *Faust* as the last resort.

HE. This is the last resort.

SHE. Nobody wants to buy this old *Faust.*

HE. That's because it's in German. And nobody wants to buy the caviar because it's Danish. In Poland, I asked you specifically to get Russian caviar. [HE*'s* *looking for the pills.*] The restaurant is called the Russian Tea Room, not the Danish Tea Room.

SHE. Don't look there, you won't find them there. [*The sound of a fire siren again. It is a slightly different sound.* HE *finds pills.*]

SHE. That's not ours. Yesterday a pigeon tried to peck my eyes out.

HE. Oh, my God, go to sleep.

SHE. I went out to buy some milk and left the window open . . .

HE. I told you, always close the windows before you go out.

SHE. I came back and there was this pigeon sitting on this table pecking at a potato . . . I went over to it, the pigeon looked directly at me, spread its wings, opened its beak, and hissed.

HE. Hissed? You mean, cooed?

SHE. Not cooed, hissed. Then he raised up one of its legs with claws on it . . .

HE. Claws?

SHE. Claws. It tried to peck my eyes out.

HE. [*in despair, without the will to resist*] Oh, my God.

SHE. I got scared. And then the pigeon stopped pecking at the potato and slowly hopped over to the window. But you know, I understand that pigeon. It has to be like that. It wouldn't survive otherwise. And I wanted to tell you that everybody's got to behave like that pigeon. Scientists have proved that New York babies are born with thicker eardrums, smaller lungs, and more hair in their noses than the average Colorado baby. So as to muffle the sound and inhale less air. You see, they naturally acquire an antipollution defense system.

They grow more hair in their noses, the windpipe through which the air goes to their lungs gets shorter, their skin becomes thicker and their nails harder. That's what the latest research has shown. [HE *turns light out.*]

HE. Let's go to sleep.

SHE. My tooth hurts. This one here. [SHE *points to it.*]

HE. That means someone in your family will get sick.

SHE. It hurts a lot.

HE. Take an aspirin. There are four left. [SHE *turns light on.*]

SHE. I have to go to the dentist.

HE. Take two now and two more in an hour.

SHE. It's a front tooth.

HE. Don't get upset. Teeth often hurt when you're under nervous stress.

SHE. You said that Zbyszek promised to lend us two hundred dollars . . . Go ask him.

HE. OK, I'll go.

SHE. Go today.

HE. OK, I'll go.

SHE. Hey, you should write a play about Zbyszek. He worked in a shipyard in Gdansk, then he got arrested, was beaten up, sent to prison. He managed to escape, when they caught him they said, prison, or leave the country. He came to America and now he's got a job renovating the Statue of Liberty . . .

HE. It sounds like socialist realism.

SHE. Americans will love it.

HE. Who'll be interested in that? Maybe if he were Russian.

SHE. OK, so make him a Russian . . . Just imagine a vicious snowstorm, full moon, the waves are rolling, and he's standing right in the torch at the top of the Statue of Liberty, singing . . . in Russian. Now that's something for Broadway. I've got to go to the dentist.

HE. Look how lucky Zbyszek was. They knocked his teeth out in prison. Now he doesn't have any more problems with the dentist.

SHE. I'm worried about our apartment in Warsaw.

HE. Why? They took it away from us.

[*They lie for several moments trying to sleep. Two plain-clothes policemen crawl out from under the bed. The first one* [RYSIO] *stocky and grim. The second* [CZESIO] *talk-ative.*]

RYSIO. It's clean under the bed, nothing suspicious there. [*dusts himself off*]

SHE. Have you got a search warrant?

CZESIO. But who's conducting a search here? Don't take it to heart, Rysiu. Rise above it, let them be insulting if they want to. How do you like the apartment, Rysiu?

RYSIO. [*contemptuously*] It stinks.

CZESIO. Don't turn up your nose, Rysiu. It's in the best part of Warsaw. Three rooms with a kitchen, and the windows have a southern exposure, don't they?

SHE. That's right, but just what are you getting at?

RYSIO. The terrace is too small.

CZESIO. Don't be so fussy, Rysiu. Look at how big the bedroom is. [HE *whistles.*]

RYSIO. After work, a guy wants to sit on the terrace with a bottle, have a drink, and think life over.

SHE. Stop it, will you.

CZESIO. The layout is not half bad. Look, you can take those bookshelves out, and you've got plenty of room.

RYSIO. It stinks. That villa that belonged to the doctor suited me better. It had a garden.

CZESIO. The captain has his eye on the villa. I'm telling you, you'd better take it. For a writer, you're pretty good at whistling, pal. That's what makes artists artists.

SHE. Look here, we were searched two weeks ago. [RYSIO *starts to emit strange sounds.*] What's wrong with him?

CZESIO. Nothing, that's just the way he laughs.

RYSIO. Can I rough her up a bit?

CZESIO. Take it easy, Rysiu, it's not worth getting worked up. My God, you'd think we were dealing with some real slobs, but she's a famous actress, a great artist. When we were going through that architect's apartment on Miodowa Street this morning he started acting up. So Rysiu roughed him up a bit, and you know what, my friends, it's hard to believe that a supposedly cultured man with the benefit of a college education would scream like that: we felt embarrassed for him.

SHE. What apartment are you two talking about? If you've got this apartment in mind let me point out that this apartment's taken, that should be obvious.

CZESIO. What's the point of pretending? I mean, why all this make-believe? Can't we talk this over like grown-ups? I mean, isn't it obvious you're going on a long trip?

SHE. Where to?

CZESIO. You're emigrating.

SHE. I don't know what you're talking about.

CZESIO. All the Jews are leaving.

SHE. We're not Jews.

CZESIO. We are the ones to decide that.

RYSIO. Excuse me, please, can I use your phone? [SHE *laughs and shrugs her shoulders.*]

CZESIO. Just what are you scribbling there, pal? Maybe you want to lodge a written complaint against us, eh? [*amused*] Hear that, Rysiu?

RYSIO. Woof! Woof!

CZESIO. Give your wife a hug from me.

RYSIO. The sarge says hello. He'd like to shake your shaggy little paw. . . . The wife sends her best greetings . . . I can hardly hear you, my pet.

CZESIO. That's because the line is bugged. Dial 11 and get them to turn it off for a while.

RYSIO. I'll call you right back, my pet.

CZESIO. How can anyone live in a country like this? Ransacking people's apartments, censorship, a total lack of freedom and justice, erosion of one's moral principles. Whereas you'll be sitting pretty in New York, living it up in Manhattan, all the Scotch you can drink . . . And the CIA finances the whole thing, lunch with Susan Sontag, then in the evening as it's getting dark the aliens come down on flying saucers. I wouldn't mind going there myself, but somebody has to stay here and maintain order . . .

RYSIO. Hello, Lieutenant Marciniak? Sergeant Rysio speaking. Listen, stop bugging the number I'm calling from for a half-hour, OK? Yeah, the terrace's too small. Thanks.

[RYSIO *calls his wife.* RYSIO *and* CZESIO *speak simultaneously.*]

RYSIO. Hello pet! Yes, now I can hear you perfectly, honey.

CZESIO. Of course, it's a terrible loss for the country. A real brain drain . . . all those scientists and artists going abroad.

RYSIO. Yeah, there are four big rooms . . .

CZESIO. It's like chopping off your own hand . . .

RYSIO. Excuse me, lady, the wife wants to know if the heating works good in winter? [SHE *nods affirmatively.*] She says it works good. But there aren't any cabinets in the kitchen.

CZESIO. There was this artist—he said he loved his country and he refused to leave, and then all of a sudden it turns out that he was a Japanese spy. He got twenty-five years. Ever been to Japan?

HE. No, only to Bulgaria.

RYSIO. The windows are large, some of them double. And there's a TV set. Excuse me, but the wife wants to know if it's a color TV?

SHE. It's black and white.

RYSIO. How come? [SHE *shrugs her shoulders. Rysio on the phone, very disappointed*] Listen my pet, I'm sorry to say it's black and white, can you imagine that! [CZESIO *turns on TV set.*]

VOICE OF THE ANNOUNCER. Yesterday a tiny band of twenty thousand CIA agents disguised as workers came out on the streets of Warsaw, brandishing emblems of the long-defunct trade union SOLIDARITY and displaying petty bourgeois anti-socialist slogans demanding bread, meat, the reduction of prices, and the establishment of equality and justice. The outraged citizens of Warsaw on their own initiative called for the forces of law and order to use water cannons and tear gas to disperse the mob . . .

RYSIO. The picture's good, honey . . .

CZESIO. There's just a little distortion, wait, I'll try the other channel . . . [CZESIO *changes the channel.*]

VOICE OF ANNOUNCER. . . . demanding bread, meat, the reduction of prices, and the establishment of equality and justice. The outraged citizens of Warsaw on their own initiative called for the forces of law and order to use water cannons and tear gas to disperse the mob . . .

RYSIO. Yes, now it's much better. Gotta get back to work. [CZESIO *turns the TV off.*]

HE. I'm not leaving anywhere. I have a right to stay here. [*the whistle of the teapot*] I'm going to make some tea.

CZESIO. Could we have a cup of tea too before we leave? [HE *gives out the tea bags for* CZESIO, RYSIO, *then gets two cups for* HE *and* SHE *and pours the water.*]

RYSIO. [*to* SHE] The wife wanted me to ask you for your autograph. We've seen all your movies, you're wearing the same nightgown.

HE. Sign it for her.

SHE. [*signing the autograph*] What's your wife's first name?

RYSIO. Katarzyna. [HE *prepares tea for himself and for* SHE. *The foursome sitting on the bed in total silence dip their tea bags in their cups, keeping the same rhythm and tempo.*]

CZESIO. Look, it's Lipton's. You know I really like you, just tell me one thing. You look smart, why do you write?

HE. Why? [*They stop dipping tea bags.*]

CZESIO. A smart man never writes, a smart man never leaves any trace behind him. [RYSIO *and* CZESIO *crawl under the bed, taking their tea along with them.*]

SHE. When they came, we had no idea we were going to emigrate. [HE *nods affirmatively.*] But *they* already knew. I wonder how?

CZESIO. [*disappearing under the bed*] Rysiu, did you hear that? She wonders how we knew. [RYSIO's *peculiar laugh can be heard from beneath the bed.*]

SHE. [SHE *begins to massage his back, kisses him.*] Listen, why don't you call that director?

HE. You mean John?

SHE. He really liked your last play, he wanted to do something with it.

HE. Oh, you're just saying that.

SHE. He really is a good director.

HE. Oh, come on, what's the point of it, it's a waste of time talking to him. The guy's a nervous wreck, he can't pull himself together. He hasn't been able to finish anything for the past few years. He's finished creatively. They say he hasn't been able to get a decent night's sleep for over two years! He's Czechoslovakian. [SHE *continues sensual massage, kisses him.*] Oh, no. I'm not going to fall for that. [HE *tries to get out of her clutches,* SHE *holds him tight. They struggle.*]

SHE. What's the matter?

HE. Oh no. I know very well what's on your mind.

SHE. [HE *tries to get out of her grip, but* SHE *holds him tight, pushing against the iron headboard of the bed. While the struggle continues, they carry on their conversation.*] What would be the harm in having a baby?

HE. Where would we put it?

SHE. Over there.

HE. And what about us?

SHE. Over here.

HE. Where would I do my writing?

SHE. You're not doing any writing.

HE. I have nothing to write about.

SHE. Write about me.

HE. About you?

SHE. About me.

HE. But what about you?

SHE. Write what you think about me.

HE. There is nothing interesting about you.

SHE. OK. So write what you really think about me.

HE. It wouldn't make any difference.

SHE. If you'd only written a sentence a day, it would have amounted to three hundred sixty-five times three years, minus Sunday, nine hundred thirty-nine sentences, that makes at least the first act of a play. [*addressing the audience directly*] No?

BLACKOUT

Act Two

[SHE'*s lying under the sheets.* HE'*s in a chair studying the map; nearby is a can of roach spray.*]

HE. What a strange country. I was born in a town that was Polish once, then it was Czech, then it was Austrian, then it was Russian, then it was German, and now it's Communist. When Stalin died, during a memorial ceremony at our school the principal informed us that the leaders of the Polish People's Republic had decided to honor the memory of the best friend Polish children ever had by renaming our school *Stalinowka* and the town to Stalinowo. So I suggested our principal also be renamed Joseph Stalin. The colonel in the Secret Police who interrogated me really liked the idea of renaming our principal to Stalin. I was lucky. He not only saved me from prison but he showed a lot of interest in my career, until he was transferred to Rome as an expert on religious affairs.

During the darkest years of Stalinism, when I was a little boy, my father took me to see an exhibit entitled "This is America" at Dzerzhinsky Square in Warsaw. Feliks Dzerzhinsky, a Polish national hero, was the first chief of the Soviet KGB, when it was still known as the Cheka. The protagonist of many socialist plays and films, he was well known for his affection for young children, though he often had a deadly dislike for parents.

The exhibition at the square named for him displayed loud ties, gaudy billboards, burning crosses of the KKK, and even bugs from Colorado that were trained at special camps to be dropped from planes at night to devour socialists' potatoes. All this to a decadent boogie-woogie soundtrack.

The exhibition was meant to evoke horror, disgust, and hatred. It had, however, the opposite effect. Thousands of Varsovians, dressed in their holiday best, waited every day in lines as long as those to see Lenin's Tomb and in solemn silence looked at the display, listened respectfully to the boogie-woogie, wanting in this way, at least, to manifest their blind and hopeless love for the United States. [*demonstrates*] Here's France, and Austria, and Germany, the Soviet Union, Poland. The boundary lines between all the countries twist, and turn, and twitch like worms in a can. Messy. [*points to the map*] That's what you call a neat job. Look here. [*points to states on the map and then to other states, all of which are rectangular in shape, making appropriate gestures all the while*] Montana, Wyoming, North Dakota, South Dakota . . . Missouri [HE *pronounces it "misery"*]. This country was laid out by someone who had technical training. [SHE *appears.*] Buildings, [*traces rectangles in the air*] streets, [*traces lines*] everything, even people are well made. That's what you'd call a good piece of work. Only the cockroaches seem not to have come out quite right . . . yet.

SHE. You're not going to use that, are you? [HE *crosses away from the map.*] It's a terrible poison. You know Małgosia. The most successful Polish actress ever. She was a bartender at this little bar on the corner of Seventh Street and First Avenue. They happened to be making a Miller beer commercial there. And they went into ecstasies over her. Shortly afterward she married a producer, then she left him for another producer. Now she's got a role in a full-length movie, is modeling for *Vogue.* Do you know what she told me? She told me never to use that spray. She personally uses only that white powder sprinkled evenly along the walls. The powder poisons them slowly, dazes them. They start moving slower and slower, and slower. The powder eats through their shell. And then they start reeling like drunks and then they die. It kills the eggs too. And to think that when I played Lady Macbeth in Warsaw, she was only the third witch. [HE *turns out light.*] I was in the park yesterday.

HE. We stayed home all day long yesterday. The last time we went out was Sunday.

SHE. I was in the park Sunday.

HE. What for?

SHE. It was dark already.

HE. What park?

SHE. In our park. The Tompkins Square Park between Avenue A and B. [HE *turns light on.*]

HE. You mean to tell me you actually went in the park after dark?

SHE. That's right.

HE. I don't believe you.

SHE. The place was swarming with people.

HE. I know, and the only thing you're afraid of is empty streets. What have you got against empty streets? If there's no one on the street, no one is going to harm you. Do you remember that time on Orchard Street you were so scared because it was absolutely empty? Then you breathed a sign of relief when at last you spotted a human being. And that was the human being who mugged us. How could you go in the park after dark?

SHE. They think the park is quite safe.

HE. What they?

SHE. The people who live in the park.

HE. How am I supposed to do any writing if you keep telling me things like that?

SHE. I went to the park because you don't do any writing.

HE. Didn't anyone bother you?

SHE. No.

HE. You were lucky. [HE *turns light out.*]

SHE. But I picked up someone. [HE *turns light on.*]

HE. What for?

SHE. Out of fear.

HE. Fear of what?

SHE. That we're going to end up in the park eventually.

HE. The park is populated only by crazy people, drunks, drug addicts, and gangsters.

SHE. No, the gangsters are in Chicago.

BUM. [*The voice of the* BUM *coming from under the bed*] Neurosis.

HE. What?

[*The* BUM *starts to crawl out from under the bed.*]

BUM. Your wife is neurotic. [*He climbs onto the bed and starts to scratch himself.*] Just take a look at her. You should be more considerate of her feelings. I don't think she's happy.

HE. Why?

BUM. Last night I saw her in the park talking to herself.

HE. Yesterday we stayed home all day long.

BUM. You're right. I saw her last Sunday. [*scratches himself more and more energetically*] Don't worry, it's the mange, not fleas.

HE. Oh, I see.

BUM. You don't look too peppy yourself. Do you booze?

HE. No, I just can't sleep.

BUM. Too bad. I thought you might have a small bottle hidden away somewhere.

HE. So you're an alcoholic.

BUM. That's right. Bedspreads are all right, but after two days of steady rain, they're finished. Disposable items are always preferable. [*points to back issues of the* Times *scattered all over the room*] Take these foot warmers along. [BUM *wraps paper around Jan's feet.* HE *eyes the foot warmers dubiously, walks about trying them out.*] It's a very wise decision on your part. Why are you afraid of living in the park, children? Our park, it's the best park in the city. The only ideal location, if you plan to stay in Manhattan, of course.

SHE. What are you talking about? What park? What do you need any park for? We've got an apartment. We're paying rent . . . [*The* BUM *lifts his head up and looks at her questioningly.*] Well, as a matter of fact, we are behind on our payment but only for the last month's rent . . . [*After a moment, the* BUM *looks up again.*] . . . OK, for the last two months . . . Besides, Zbyszek has promised to lend us the last two months.

BUM. [*pointing to the TV set*] Oh, there's my stool. [*He gets up from the bed and sits on the TV set.*]

SHE. You're smashing our TV set.

BUM. This stool of mine stood for an entire week on the corner of Fifth Street and Avenue B.

HE. I told you we shouldn't have taken that TV set off the street. I knew we'd get into trouble because of it.

SHE. Don't butt into this, I'm going to deal with him . . . All right, I admit it, I took that TV set off the street. I'm not the least ashamed to have *one* item in my apartment that was picked out of the trash on the sidewalk. [*The* BUM *taps on the chair with his finger.*] Well, OK, maybe two items. [*The* BUM *points to the table.*]

SHE. And the table, so what?! Most young couples in New York furnish their apartments out of the trash found on the sidewalks. Thanks to that [*points to TV set*] we could watch the birthday party for the Statue of Liberty.

BUM. It's a good thing you chose our park. A lot of beginners are taken in by the charms of Central Park.

SHE. I already told you we're not going to any park. [*Meanwhile* HE *turns his back on the* BUM *and puts the blanket over his head.*]

BUM. To be perfectly honest with you, the view in Central Park is better, but the police there wake you up all the time and push your feet off the bench, and make you smile for the tourists taking pictures. You're under a lot of stress there.

SHE. *[to Jan]* What are you up to?

HE. I'm ignoring him.

SHE. Well, do something.

HE. Let's go to bed and pretend he's not here. Come close and pull the covers up! [SHE *gets into bed next to him. They pull the covers up.*]

BUM. The people who go to live in Central Park run out of steam after a month or two. And move to Washington Square, but sooner or later, when they can't keep it up any longer, they end up in our park.

HE. *[from under the covers]* That's what comes of your clever ideas about picking people up.

SHE. *[from under the covers]* I can't take it any longer.

HE. *[from under the covers]* Let's show him we've got class.

SHE. *[from under the covers]* Look, I'm shaking all over.

HE. *[from under the covers]* Don't let yourself be taken in. Just keep calm. [*Suddenly* HE *jumps up in a rage, tossing the covers aside.*] What's going on here? I have a lecture in the morning. Stop talking all that rubbish. You don't have any right to be here.

SHE. Calm down.

HE. *[runs over to the wardrobe]* Look over here. [HE *struggles with it, without being able to open the door.*]

BUM. A cabinet like that should be attacked from the bottom. Then it'll open. [*Jan follows the* BUM's *instructions in attacking the door. The wardrobe opens.* HE *looks for something inside.*] That cabinet used to be located between Second and Third Street at Avenue C. I used it in October when it rained so much. [*Meanwhile Jan finds his jacket and takes his wallet out of the pocket.* HE *goes over to the* BUM.]

HE. Look at this. It's my PEN membership card. This is for the Dramatists Guild, and this is for the Authors League of America.

BUM. Sssshhhh. Did you hear that?

HE. What was it?

BUM. A Mercedes just went by. That's the second one this week. I've sighted a BMW recently.

HE. [*lowering his voice*] Are you afraid of the Germans too?

BUM. The neighborhood is getting gentrified. They are going to clean up the park. [*His eyes darting about, the* BUM *comes forward to the front of the stage, crouches behind a chair, pulls a pint bottle of liquor out of his hip pocket, and takes a gulp.*]

SHE. Oh, my God . . . Zyrardow . . .

HE. Are you starting that all over again?

SHE. [SHE *goes over to the* BUM, *falls to her knees on the other side of the chair, and continues talking as though at confession.*] My mother used to send my father out to get water from the street pump. We were hopelessly poor. We lived in Zyrardow on Victory of the Revolution Street. Father would take the bucket and go straight to the bar on Glorious Future Street. He'd check his bucket in the cloakroom. There'd always be about thirty buckets hanging there on the hooks. At midnight they'd close the bar and that's when my mother would send me to get Father. I was fourteen then. One night when I was dragging Father home, he pretended not to know who I was. That was on St.

Marks . . . I mean, Karl Marx Street. There were no streetlights and it was always so dark.

HE. You see what you've done to my wife? Who are you anyway? What did you come here for? [*The* BUM *looks through his pockets for something.*]

SHE. Five years ago a journalist from *Der Stern* asked me whether I'd like to be fourteen years old again. Those Germans can't get Faust out of their heads. But it put me into a cold sweat. I told him that would be the worst joke life could play on me. A person's got the strength to make such a climb only once in a lifetime. [*The* BUM *pulls something out of his pocket that looks like an ID card wrapped in several layers of paper napkins. He hands the bundle to* HE. HE *starts to unwrap it with great care.*]

SHE. In my case, this remake of *Faust* doesn't work very well. The devil was furious because I left Poland. I refused to make a deal with him. So in revenge he screwed up my brain. Now here I am . . . fourteen again and back in Zyrardow. I've lost everything except my accent. [HE *finishes the unwrapping, revealing the content of the bundle. It is an empty plastic case, the dimensions of an ID card.*]

HE. There's nothing in it.

BUM. [*checks for himself and agrees with Jan*] That's right. [*He takes the plastic cover out of Jan's hand, carefully rewrapping it in the paper napkins, then puts it back in his pocket. Next he starts to crawl slowly under the bed.*] Your wife will calm down once you're in the park. [*to* SHE] Hold out your hands. [*to* HE] See?

SHE. See what? [SHE *looks at her hands, which don't shake.*]

BUM. What do you mean, see what?

SHE. Are they shaking?

HE. I don't know. Maybe not. Maybe just a little.

BUM. [*ironically*] Is that what you call "just a little"? When I first moved to our park, my nerves were just like yours. Now take a look at my hands. [*The* BUM *stretches out both hands, which shake terribly. Triumphantly*] How about that?

HE. I don't know. How can I put it . . .

SHE. Your hands are shaking.

BUM. Are you kidding? [*He looks at* HE, *who nods in consent. Astounded*] Do you really think so?

HIM. Can't you see for yourself?

BUM. [*looking at his hands*] Well, maybe just a little bit. That's nothing. You should have seen my hands before. They'll straighten out once I get back to the park, you'll see. [*disappears under the bed*]

SHE. Oh, God. Maybe he knows that we'll end up in the park.

HE. How could he know that?

SHE. [*looking at her hands*] How did those secret policemen know we were going to leave Poland? Go see Zbyszek right away. Ask him to lend us money to pay the rent. [HE *fails to react.*] Did you hear? [HE *whistles.*] What's going on?

HE. He won't lend us any money.

SHE. He promised he would.

HE. You see, it seems Zbyszek didn't have a work permit.

SHE. What do you mean he didn't have a work permit?

HE. He was using a forged card. Strictly illegal. He and a Turkish worker.

SHE. Good God.

HE. Someone turned them in as illegal aliens. Immigration officers raided the Statue of Liberty and arrested Zbyszek and the Turk, in the torch. [HE *shakes his head negatively.*]

SHE. But if they send Zbyszek back to Poland, he'll be put in jail immediately.

HE. Maybe not immediately.

SHE. Janek . . .

HE. Yes?

SHE. Maybe it's punishment.

HE. What punishment?

SHE. That we can't sleep . . . Punishment for running away from Poland.

HE. Nonsense. They threw us out.

SHE. We could've resisted . . . Janek . . .

HE. What now?

SHE. Maybe we should pray.

HE. What?

SHE. But why not? Let's just try. It wouldn't hurt. I mean, the Pope is a Pole.

HE. But God isn't.

SHE. Let's pray.

HE. What an idea!

SHE. Do it for me. As a favor. [*They awkwardly try to find a place to kneel.*]

HE. OK. What language should we pray in? In Polish or in English?

SHE. It doesn't make any difference.

HE. I don't know how to pray in English.

SHE. Let's start with "Our Father who art in heaven . . ."

HE. What are we praying for?

SHE. For us to fall asleep.

HE. Maybe . . .

SHE. What?

HE. Let's start with something easier than that . . . if it works then we'll ask for more.

SHE. For a green card.

HE. Think so?

SHE. Sure! [*They both concentrate on praying.*]

HE. [*after a moment*] I can't.

SHE. But why not?

HE. Oh Christ!

SHE. For God's sake don't be sacrilegious.

HE. I'm ashamed to pray for a green card. [HE *turns out the light.*]

SHE. No Janek. You can't give up. Listen, this is America. [*chasing a cockroach*] Ugh . . . [SHE *squashes it by pounding it with her shoe against the floor. From the floor below comes the sound of pounding on the ceiling with the broom.*

HE. Oh, damn. A knocking from below.

SHE. So what. It means we haven't fallen to the very bottom yet. At least somebody is still below us.

HE. Strange it didn't occur to me until now. Of course, in Milton and Baudelaire termites, sometimes other insects, rhythmically beat their heads against the floor to inform the hero of his imminent death. In Genet too . . . You appeared in Genet's plays, do you remember?

SHE. I don't think the cockroaches would warn us. And you know that it's the old hag downstairs who keeps knocking.

HE. In Goethe's *Faust* knocking precedes the coming of Mephistopheles from hell.

SHE. But she's from Lithuania. [*in desperation*] Why

don't you write? Dear God, just think, a morbid brain like yours is being wasted. We could afford to buy a house if you only knew how to sell those obsessions of yours. It you can't write a full-length book, write something, one line at least, something to the point like "McDonald's—we do it all for you." It might be that our bed is standing over a vein of water which alters the magnetic field, and that in turn causes our insomnia. Let's change the position of the bed . . .

HE. We already did that only yesterday.

SHE. Let's do it again. The vein of water can change its course and follow every move we make . . . I bought you that book, *Money Is My Friend,* and you haven't even opened it yet.

HE. You didn't buy it, you found it in the trash. You expect me to learn how to make money by reading a book which someone else threw out in the garbage.

SHE. Maybe that person had already made his money and got rid of the book when he didn't need it anymore.

HE. I wanted to tell you that at first when I arrived in America I was self-possessed, I tried hard, if only you'd behaved differently.

SHE. I did everything you asked me to. You said one can't get anywhere in America without being in the phone book, so I took care of it. *I* took care of it. We're in the phone book, Krupinski, only no one calls us.

HE. Please do forgive me, but I'd like to remind you that it was due to me, and to all the time and effort that I put into it, that the Thompsons ever came to

visit us. And you know that they're friends with
. . .

SHE. [*interrupting him*] You're not going to start that
over again, are you?

HE. I kept begging you to get a grip on yourself. And
at least for that one evening to behave decently. I
mean, you know they're very close to . . .

SHE. [*interrupting him*] You asked me to do something
quite different.

HE. What'd I ask you to do?

SHE. To keep my mouth shut and not to say anything
bad about socialism, Jaruzelski, Gorbachev, and
the Soviet Union.

HE. If you say bad things about it, they'll say you're a
classic example of paranoia affecting émigrés.

SHE. If I say good things about them, they'll ask me
why I left Poland.

HE. I ask you not to say *anything* on the subject, only
to make a good impression. That's all. The
Thompsons are good people on whom a lot depends. They could change our entire life, they
could help us find a publisher for my new book,
they could introduce us to . . .

SHE. What new book? I think . . .

HE. You can think anything you want, but just don't
say it.

SHE. The Secret Police in Poland said exactly the same
thing.

HE. Just who do you think you are? The conscience of
the nation?

[*An American couple crawl out from under the bed. They
are both very elegantly dressed, in evening clothes.* MR.

THOMPSON *brings with him two folded blankets in a plastic bag.* MRS. THOMPSON, *who is trying unsuccessfully to conceal her fear of the surroundings, carries a small, beautifully wrapped gift. As the* THOMPSONS *appear from under the bed, the conversation in the room is drawing to a close.*]

HE. And please, don't change.

SHE. Why?

HE. You look fine just as you are.

SHE. Why?

HE. You should look totally natural.

SHE. Why?

HE. To arouse their compassion. [SHE *disappears into the bathroom, slamming the door.* HE *puts on a jacket and glasses.* HE, *turning to the* THOMPSONS] I'm so glad you've come. We really appreciate it that you found the time to drop by and pay us a visit. Welcome, welcome.

MR. THOMPSON. [*picking the two folded blankets in a plastic bag off the floor*] No, no, it's up to us to welcome you to America. Welcome, welcome. You look wonderful. Last time I saw you, you had me somewhat worried. Right, dear?

MRS. THOMPSON. Oh, yes. [*Exchange of handshakes, during which Jan's hand leaves ink smudges on the* THOMPSON'*s hands.* MR. THOMPSON *pretends he doesn't notice anything while* MRS. THOMPSON *tries to wipe the ink off with a handkerchief.*]

HE. They took our fingerprints. For the green card. They of course suspect us of being spies.

MR. THOMPSON. Of course. I mean . . . I'm sorry to hear that. All these formalities are so awful.

HE. I don't know. It's not so bad. It's just difficult to get the ink off afterward.

MRS. THOMPSON. [*with growing fear in her eyes, speaking unnaturally loudly as if to make her English understandable*] It's a very nice apartment.

HE. We're still furnishing it. We're going to put an armchair over there, and a rug here. And a chair somewhere.

MRS. THOMPSON. It's already very nice and cozy as it is. Besides, I read in the *Times* that the neighborhood is getting better . . . and better.

HE. Oh, yes, yes, the neighborhood. My wife's in the bathroom. Excuse me, I'll go get something to drink. Make yourselves at home.

MRS. THOMPSON. Oh, that's very nice of you. I'd just like a cup of tea, please. [*Her eyes rest on the used tea bags hanging on the rope to dry.*] Or just a glass of water.

HE. Of course, right away.

MR. THOMPSON. If you'd seen our first apartment, my dear boy. Am I right, dear? [MRS. THOMPSON *bursts out in nervous laughter.*]

MR. THOMPSON. I have the feeling you'll make it here. [HE *is busy in the kitchen.*]

MRS. THOMPSON. Did you see those people in front of the building? I'm afraid they'll break into our car.

MR. THOMPSON. You can't judge people by appearances.

MRS. THOMPSON. I know, but I left my fur coat in the car. Good God, take a look at that bathtub.

MR. THOMPSON. Sshhh. You've got to be very careful of what you say, dear, or you'll hurt their feelings.

MRS. THOMPSON. Look, there's not a single painting.

MR. THOMPSON. But they're very brave. I'm sure they'll get a painting soon. And please, dear, don't say good things about socialism in their presence.

MRS. THOMPSON. [*astonished*] But socialism is a noble idea!

MR. THOMPSON. I know, dear, I know. But they've suffered a lot over there. And if they say something good about Reagan, don't be upset.

MRS. THOMPSON. What do you mean?

MR. THOMPSON. [*soothingly; looks around*] Yes, we'll invite them over some day soon. We'll introduce them to . . . It's our moral responsibility. They are interesting people. There's a sense of mystery about them. For example, he's written such a strange, dark novel.

MRS. THOMPSON. But you haven't even read it.

MR. THOMPSON. I'll read it during my vacation.

HE. [*to* MR. THOMPSON] I'm awfully sorry, I don't know what happened, I'd like to do something to help, but a bottle of vodka got misplaced somewhere. Oh, I've got some sleeping pills. I hid them from my wife somewhere. [HE *bustles around the bed, finds a bottle of sleeping pills and offers it to the* THOMPSONS.] Here they are. But you don't have any trouble sleeping, do you?

MRS. THOMPSON. I didn't know your wife suffers from insomnia.

HE. No, no, it's nothing serious. My wife and I always sleep at the same times.

MRS. THOMPSON. That's wonderful.

HE. [*in Polish*] Wyjdziesz wreszcie, czy nie. Oni zaraz sobie podją.

MR. THOMPSON. By the way, we brought you two blan-

kets which might come in handy sometime. And
. . . a small nothing, more symbolic than anything
else. [MRS. THOMPSON *hands to* HE *an elegantly
wrapped replica of the Statue of Liberty. He unwraps
it and examines it enraptured, then places it along
several identical ones.*]

MRS. THOMPSON. I've heard that your wife is an actress.

MR. THOMPSON. My wife knows a lot of people in the
theater. We'll try to help.

HE. That'd be wonderful. [*shouts*] Anka, hurry up, will
you?

MRS. THOMPSON. What kind of roles does she appear
in?

HE. Mainly the classical repertory. Women in Shakespeare.

MR. THOMPSON. Women in Shakespeare . . . Then
we've definitely got to call Joe.

MRS. THOMPSON. Has your wife got an accent?

HE. [*proudly*] Of course. She doesn't have a work permit. But she's got an accent.

MRS. THOMPSON. Well, after all no one knows what
Elizabethan English actually sounded like.

HE. That'd be wonderful. [*knocks at the bathroom door*]

MR. THOMPSON. Is your wife a member of Equity?

HE. I don't know about that.

MRS. THOMPSON. Of course in order to perform in
New York your wife first has to become a member
of Equity. But of course in order to become a
member of Equity your wife must have performed
in New York.

HE. [*confused*] Of course.

MRS. THOMPSON. There is a certain way of circumventing this regulation. I mean it could be done as a cultural exchange between our two governments. Let's say your wife would go back to Poland . . . let's say for one year, and the Polish government would arrange a performance for her in New York, at the same time inviting as a cultural exchange an outstanding American actress to perform in Warsaw. Meryl Streep! She's got a terrific Polish accent.

HE. But we have emigrated from Poland.

MRS. THOMPSON. Yes. That can be an obstacle.

MR. THOMPSON. Tell me quite frankly, what do you think of us?

HE. What do I think of you?

MR. THOMPSON. You can be straight with me. [*Pause. They look at each other.*] Do you like America?

HE. Oh, we think it's a great country and wonderful too.

MR. THOMPSON. Of course. But you must understand that not everything in America is as wonderful as it looks.

HE. No?

MR. THOMPSON. No. You see, all the émigrés who come here are above all grateful, as you yourself noticed, for the boundless opportunities and for the sense of freedom and security that America offers them. That's only understandable.

HE. I should say so.

MR. THOMPSON. I'm connected with a publishing house which is interested in a slightly different view of America. A more complex view, a more probing view . . . a darker view, if you will . . .

HE. I will . . .

MR. THOMPSON. . . . a view which would show us what we Americans have lost . . . For I am of the opinion that you émigrés have got something that we don't.

HE. We do?

MR. THOMPSON. Yes, you do.

HE. What's that?

MR. THOMPSON. A soul.

HE. A soul?

MR. THOMPSON. A soul. I've mentioned your name to the publisher. Are you interested?

HE. In writing a book about having a soul?

MR. THOMPSON. No, a book about not having a soul.

HE. I'm definitely interested. Do you think they'll give me an advance immediately?

MR. THOMPSON. [*somewhat irritated*] Submit a chapter or two first . . . I'm sure you'll write it in no time at all. I can imagine with all the new impressions you've been gathering, you must be a volcano of energy.

HE. [*clenching his fists energetically*] Oh, yes.

MR. THOMPSON. You looked around the streets. Haven't you noticed?

HE. Yes, there is something I haven't seen. But it's a lot of wonderful things . . .

MR. THOMPSON. [*correcting him*] The dark side.

HE. Yes, absolutely!

MR. THOMPSON. Look at the subway.

HE. I agree. The graffiti for example. It's hooliganism. In Poland they would never allow it.

MR. THOMPSON. I'm afraid that here I have to disagree. Graffiti is a popular form of a true folk art which expresses the soul.

HE. The soul?

MR. THOMPSON. In certain places we still have some left.

MRS. THOMPSON. [*screams*] Aaaa . . .

MR. THOMPSON. What happened?

HE. What happened?

MRS. THOMPSON. Nothing, absolutely nothing, everything's all right. I simply need a glass of water.

HE. I'll get it for you right away. [*runs over to the kitchen*]

MR. THOMPSON. What was it, dear?

MRS. THOMPSON. There's a rat under the bed.

MR. THOMPSON. What do you mean a rat?

MRS. THOMPSON. A rat. [*screams*] Look, there it is! [*points with her finger*]

HE. [*returning with a glass of water in his hand*] Did something happen?

MR. THOMPSON. No, nothing at all. Just a rat who ran under the bed.

HE. Oh, please, don't worry, that's not a rat, just a big mouse.

MR. THOMPSON. There, you see.

MRS. THOMPSON. [*again in an exaggeratedly loud voice*] It was a rat. It's got a very long, hairless tail.

HE. You can believe me, it's a big mouse. Mice frequently have long, hairless tails. I know what I'm talking about. I've already started a book . . .

MR. THOMPSON. Oh, that sounds wonderful.

HE. A book about a Polish writer who comes to New York and plans to kill a rich old woman who lives on Park Avenue. He argues that she has no right to go on living . . .

MRS. THOMPSON. [*appalled*] Why does he think that?

HE. [*animated*] He maintains he knows better than she does how to make use of her money. He's planning to kill her with an ax. [HE *demonstrates*. MR. *and* MRS. THOMPSON *exchange bewildered glances.*] Of course, my book owes a certain debt to Dostoyevsky. But unlike Dostoyevsky's hero, the hero in my book doesn't kill the old woman. In fact, she turns out to be a very charming old lady . . . She seduces him, he falls in love with her, and then . . . they go to this . . . this . . . Florida together . . . Because here in America the general situation and opportunities are quite different than in Russia. [*He stops a moment and notices disgust on the faces of his guests.*] I suppose it might be in bad taste, mightn't it? . . . That's why I stopped working on it.

[*The bathroom door is flung open. From inside out rolls the wheelchair with* SHE *in it.* SHE's *wearing the costume of a nineteenth-century Polish émigré. A scarf around her head. A huge shawl wrapping her body tightly; huge oversized boots, a missing front tooth. She's distinctly pregnant. A bottle of vodka in her hand. With a friendly smile she wheels the chair toward the* THOMPSONS.]

MR. THOMPSON. I'm so pleased to meet you. You look wonderful. [*He stretches out his hand.* SHE *tries to kiss it. Pulling his hand away*] I'm so pleased to meet you. [SHE *squeezes* MRS. THOMPSON's *hand, leaving ink smudges on it.*]

MR. THOMPSON. Courageous people . . . I didn't realize that your wife . . . [*Meanwhile* SHE, *making friendly gestures and patting the bottle of vodka fondly, invites them to the table, mumbling in Polish.*]

SHE. Wodka, wodka, na zdrowíe.

HE. It's nothing serious.

MR. THOMPSON. There are still many roles: *The Glass Menagerie* . . . *Sunrise at Campobello* . . . *Richard III.* [*He crawls under the bed.*]

MRS. THOMPSON. [*crawling under the bed*] I think you're going too far. Yesterday it was American Indians and now it's Polish émigrés. It's really too much.

SHE. I'm sorry but I can't stand compassion. And I really don't like suffering. And I hate that Dostoevsky of yours and all his heroes who commit frightful deeds and then with their hands folded in prayer voluntarily go off to Siberia, accept suffering, and become saints. I never wronged anyone, I don't want to suffer, and I reject feelings of compassion. [HE *takes vodka into kitchen.* SHE *speaks to audience.*] Oh, God, how very amusing I used to be when I first came to this country. I was the center of attention at parties. I'd tell jokes. Everyone would say how bright I was. I'd quote the Talmud. But now all I want to do is to cut their throats. That's why I'd like to go into business. [HE *returns.*] Anyway you could have written that chapter or two and have showed them to him. I still don't understand why you don't.

HE. What could I write about America when for over a year I haven't ventured beyond Fourth Street. [SHE *turns light on.*]

SHE. Did you know that now you can call Poland direct just by dialing the country code?

HE. So what?

SHE. And the rates are cheaper this early in the morning.

HE. How much?

SHE. $1.40 a minute.

HE. You call that cheap? $4.20 for three minutes?

SHE. No. Each additional minute is forty cents. So it'd be only $2.20 for three minutes.

HE. Only $2.20?

SHE. Let's make a call.

HE. What'll I say?

SHE. Well, I don't know. Ask them how they are. We'll do without milk for a few days. It must be about noon there now. Go ahead, just dial the code.

HE. OK.

SHE. You'll see how great it will be. Let's call Jurek. Where's my address book? [SHE *finds it and looks for the number.*]

HE. But Jurek is in Australia.

SHE. Not Jurek.

HE. Yes, Jurek. He emigrated to Australia.

SHE. Are you sure? How's he doing in Australia?

HE. He's doing very well.

SHE. Acting?

HE. He works as a gas station attendant.

SHE. That means he got a work permit. When did he leave Poland?

HE. A year ago. It's much easier to get a work permit in Australia.

SHE. What about calling Andrzej?

HE. Andrzej is in Paris.

SHE. Then how about Basia?

HE. Basia's in prison.

SHE. Maybe Bolek?

HE. Bolek hanged himself.

SHE. That's right. I knew that.

HE. Maybe Rysiek.

SHE. What are you talking about? He became a collaborator, nobody even shakes his hand now. [SHE *crosses out his name in her address book.*] Let's call Irena!

HE. That's not such a good idea.

SHE. Why not?

HE. Zbyszek called her the other day and she hung up on him. Her telephone is bugged. And besides, she just got out of the clink. She's scared and sick.

SHE. I can understand that she didn't want to talk to Zbyszek. But I was her best friend . . .

HE. You know, they say I'm working for the CIA . . .

SHE. I forgot. Maybe we should call CIA and ask them to forward our check. [SHE *picks up the telephone.*]

HE. Anyway, better not put her on the spot. She'll feel awful if she hangs up on you, and if she doesn't, she may get into trouble. [SHE *dials twelve numbers.*] Who are you calling? [SHE *doesn't answer.*] Tell me.

SHE. It's exactly 12:25 PM in Poland now. I just called.

HE. 12:25?

SHE. 12:26 now. [*Hangs up the phone. They lie for several moments in silence.*

HE. How long has it been since we stopped being able to sleep?

SHE. Shortly after we came to America, at first I couldn't sleep for something like a month, then I could, and then I couldn't again. Oh, my front tooth's hurting again . . . Since when did we stop sleeping together?

HE. Three hundred eighty-five days ago.

SHE. Are you sure you really wouldn't like to have a tiny little creature with gray-blue eyes? [HE *remains silent.*] I mean, a little kid like that would greet you every time you came home.

HE.   We don't go out anymore. [HE *gets back in bed.* SHE *follows him.*]

SHE.   But we could start going out again at night. We'd reach an agreement with the cockroaches since they sleep during the day and hunt at night. That way we wouldn't bother one another anymore. What do you think?

HE.   I wonder how cockroaches propagate?

SHE.   Come cuddle closer.

HE.   Do they make love in the normal way?

SHE.   I'm sure cockroaches go see horror movies about people, and then after the movies, they kiss and hop into bed.

HE.   I read somewhere that cockroaches are all female . . . I didn't want to tell you.

SHE.   Now you're starting all over again.

HE.   . . . and that they propagate by cellular division . . . they don't need a male.

SHE.   You're talking pure nonsense. [HE *doesn't move.*] By cellular division . . . [SHE *turns out the light and falls asleep.*]

[*The* CENSOR *appears in the middle of the bed.*]

CENSOR.   I'm from the Central Bureau of Censorship. I mean the Central Office of Human Relations. [*He smiles.*] I would like to invite you back to Poland. We will of course publish all your work.

HE.   But you took my apartment away from me.

CENSOR.   Your apartment has been renovated. Our interior decorator allowed himself to refurnish it Victorian style, which I remember, from the last

play of yours we banned, you like very much.
Haven't you heard about the changes in our country? Haven't you been reading the *New York
Times*? Your English must be good enough by
now.

HE. Wait a minute. You're not my censor. I know my
own censor, don't I?

CENSOR. You mean Tadek? Poor guy, he has been
transferred. He wasn't open-minded enough . . .
too inflexible. We are retraining him. Here are two
plane tickets for you and your wife, first class of
course! And food and gasoline coupons for the
first two years.

HE. I appreciate it very much.

CENSOR. You're very welcome.

HE. Yes, but for how long? I'm very sorry. I don't
know how to put it, but I wasn't born yesterday.
You know, I've seen it all before.

CENSOR. You've got no conscience.

HE. Yes, I do.

CENSOR. No, you've got no conscience.

HE. Maybe I've got no conscience but I've got a memory. [HE *gives the tickets back.*]

CENSOR. Maybe you've got a memory but you'll never
write anything in the States.

HE. And what makes you so sure?

CENSOR. I've gone through all your notes. They don't
lead anywhere—except maybe to the Lower East
Side. And let me tell you in confidence, two thousand dissident immigrants, all of them prominent,
have just been put on a jumbo jet in Moscow and
are leaving for New York. They are all carrying the
very same stuff you brought. I've gone through all

their notes, too. And I can tell you that they are all very talented. Whatever you say, Gogol, Dostoevsky, Tolstoy—that's some heritage! I wish all of them the best of luck. We believe that a short stay on the Lower East Side is a priceless experience for our free thinkers. [HE *gives the tickets back again.*] No! Are you sure? [CENSOR *looks around, takes off his jacket and is wearing a Hawaiian shirt underneath. He takes off his bureaucrat's glasses and replaces them with sunglasses.*] Listen—if you want to stay, let's go into business together. I know the American market. I'll be your agent. We don't want to crack up in this nasty room, do we? Call my secretary—we'll do lunch. [CENSOR *exits.* HE *turns on the light.*]

HE. Anka, Anka, wake up!

SHE. What happened?

HE. I think I had a nightmare.

SHE. That's great! That means you fell asleep. Now everything will be all right for us. Now you can start to write. [HE *lies down in the bed, gives her a dirty look, and pulls the blanket over his head.* SHE *looks at him for a moment. Then* SHE *turns to the audience.*] This is a secret but tomorrow I have this audition, well, maybe not tomorrow, I'm not quite ready yet. It's to be a stand-up comedienne . . . you know . . . like on TV . . . I have this really funny piece. OK . . . A blind man and a man with only one eye were crossing the river in a boat. The blind man did the rowing and the man with only one eye steered. In the middle of the river, the blind man accidentally swung his oar out of the water and hit the man with only one eye in his good eye. "This is the end," said the man who used to have only one eye. The blind man thought they'd reached the other shore and stepped out of the boat. [SHE *waits, smiling, for the audience's reaction, then bows several times, ending with a Shakespearean flourish. After a moment, the smiling* NARRATOR *appears on the forestage.*]

NARRATOR. We must leave our heroes at the threshold of success. Very soon the diligence, perseverance, integrity, and modesty so typical of the people from the eastern part of Europe will prevail. Our hero will receive the Pulitzer Prize and our heroine will win the hearts of Broadway audiences. I hope you have enjoyed the evening. Good night and God bless you! God bless America!

BLACKOUT

THE END

Fortinbras Gets Drunk

CHARACTERS

Fortinbras, Prince of Norway

Mortinbras, his brother

Ghost of Hamlet's Father

Ghost of Fortinbras's Father

Sternborg, Norwegian Minister of Interior

Dagny Borg, Sternborg's Niece

Eight Eyes, Sternborg's Assistant

Hamlet, Prince of Denmark

Polonius, Danish Ambassador

Guard One

Guard Two

A Couple of Minor Characters

The action takes place in the court of the Norwegian King at the same time as the events in Shakespeare's *Hamlet*.

ACT ONE   Scene 1

[*Mist and wind. Enter* GHOST *and* HAMLET]

HAMLET. Where wilt thou lead me? Speak. I'll go no
    farther.
GHOST. Mark me.
HAMLET. I will.
GHOST. I am thy father's spirit;
    Doom'd for a certain term to walk the night,
    And, for the day, confin'd to waste in fires
    Til the foul crimes done in my days of nature
    Art burnt and purg'd away. But that I am forbid
    To tell the secrets of my prison-house,
    I could a tale unfold whose lightest word
    Would harrow up thy soul; freeze thy young
    blood;
    Make thy two eyes, like stars, start from their
    spheres;
    Thy knotted and combined locks to part,
    And each particular hair to stand on end,
    Like quills upon the fretful porcupine:
    But this eternal blazon must not be
    To ears of flesh and blood. List, list, O, list!
    If thou didst ever thy dear father love—
HAMLET. O God!
GHOST. Revenge this foul and most unnatural mur-
    der!

133

HAMLET. Murder!
GHOST. Murder most foul, as in the best it is;
But this most foul, strange, and unnatural.
HAMLET. Haste me to know't that I, with wings as
        swift
    As meditation or the thoughts of love,
    May sweep to my revenge.
GHOST. I find thee apt;
    And duller shouldst thou be than the fat weed
    That roots itself in ease on Lethe wharf,
    Wouldst thou not stir in this. Now, Hamlet, hear:
    'Tis given out that, sleeping in my orchard,
    A serpent stung me; so the whole ear of Denmark
    Is by a forged process of my death
    Rankly abus'd: But know, thou noble youth,
    The serpent that did sting thy father's life
    Now wears his crown.
HAMLET. O my prophetic soul!
    My uncle!

Scene 2

[*Snow, wind, and other Nordic conditions. In the middle of
the stage is a big tree. Enter* STERNBORG, *Norwegian
Minister of Interior, about fifty, and his younger assistant,*
EIGHT EYES, *a man who sees everything, including things
which don't exist.* STERNBORG *is fighting the wind, trying
to look at a large map.*]

STERNBORG. We must be standing near the Danish
        border.
EIGHT EYES. Norway ends at those trees over there.
    Denmark's on the other side.
STERNBORG. [*shivering*] Cold, windy, snow.

EIGHT EYES. [*smiles*] I must say I love a summer like this.

STERNBORG. I'm afraid that sending that ghost to Denmark wasn't such a smart idea . . . Are you sure Hamlet's superstitious?

EIGHT EYES. Polonius swears that if the Prince so much as stumbles when he leaves Elsinore he goes back inside and won't go out again that day.

STERNBORG. I saw the King this morning. He's concerned about the Danish guerillas. [*shivering*] If Hamlet decides to lead them, it could be unpleasant.

EIGHT EYES. Why? We'll just send in the army again.

STERNBORG. Well, I know. But then there'll be raping, plundering, killing . . . It's getting embarrassing for us, having to crush them every six months.

[EIGHT EYES *massages* STERNBORG'*s shoulders and drapes his own cloak over him.*]

EIGHT EYES. What's wrong with these little countries? Why do they get upset just because we're occupying them?

STERNBORG. For them it's a matter of national pride. They lack any global perspective . . . What's Prince Hamlet up to?

EIGHT EYES. My information says that he's pacing back and forth.

STERNBORG. Doing what?

EIGHT EYES. Reading.

STERNBORG. Reading what?

EIGHT EYES. Books.

STERNBORG. What books?

EIGHT EYES. One after the other.

STERNBORG. Is he Jewish?

EIGHT EYES. No.

STERNBORG. Gay?

EIGHT EYES. No. [*pulls a bundle of papers from under his
  cloak and leafs through them in the wind*] I've got
  some portraits of him here. This one is an official
  state portrait. This one was done on the sly by one
  of our best hidden artists.

STERNBORG. Sure he's not gay? He's handsome.

EIGHT EYES. Not my type.

STERNBORG. I can't quite make out this one . . . What
  kind of haircut is that?

EIGHT EYES. Those? Those are leaves. The artist was in
  a tree when he did this sketch. But I've got a very
  interesting transcript of a top secret conversation
  between Hamlet and Horatio . . . [EIGHT EYES
  hands a sheet of paper to STERNBORG]

STERNBORG. [*reads*] "I do forget myself. I'm glad to see
  you well." . . . "I saw him once." "Indeed, my
  lord." . . . "In my mind's eye." But what is that
  supposed to mean?

EIGHT EYES. Our man wasn't in the best transcribing
  position. The ditch he was in was full of water and
  had an echo.

STERNBORG. I can't believe the luck we're having.
  First, we hire a moron who kills Hamlet's father
  instead of him.

EIGHT EYES. Apparently, they looked alike.

STERNBORG. What are you talking about? One was
  eighty and the other barely forty.

EIGHT EYES. It was very dark.

STERNBORG. [*disgusted*] Agh! Let's hope Hamlet believed our ghost's crap that his uncle killed his fa-

ther. Then he could take revenge by killing him or getting in bed with his wife.

EIGHT EYES.   But his uncle's wife is Hamlet's mother!

STERNBORG.   So what? As long as he's involved with family business, he won't mess around with the guerillas. But I'm afraid he's too smart to believe in ghosts.

EIGHT EYES.   Educated people get confused very easily. Once we get him doubting he'll get completely stuck.

STERNBORG.   We just need a little time to clean up our internal problems. His Majesty was talking to me just this morning about his sons, Fortinbras and Mortinbras. You know he doesn't trust them.

EIGHT EYES.   No?

STERNBORG.   No. And one more thing, find out why this incompetent who played the ghost dropped ten of his best lines.

DARKNESS

Scene 3

[*Snow and wind. From behind the tree, a thin arch of water crosses the stage. Suddenly, a coyotelike yet human howl is heard from offstage. Someone is hurting. The arch of water stops. From behind the tree,* GUARD ONE *appears, buttoning up his fly. He's cold and the howling isn't warming him. He pulls a bottle of vodka out from inside the tree and starts wrestling with the cap. It's stuck. He wrenches it, twists it, bites it, hits it, jumps on it, smacks it against the tree. It opens easily. Relieved and happy, he lifts the bottle to his mouth and just as he's about to take a swig the howling begins again. He chokes on his drink.*

GUARD TWO, *considerably older, appears. During their conversation, they will patrol the stage together.*]

GUARD ONE. Halt, who goes there?
GUARD TWO. No, I say that. "Halt, who goes there?"
GUARD ONE. Is that you?
GUARD TWO. Of course, it's me.

[*Another howl is heard, stopping them both in their tracks for a moment.*]

GUARD ONE. What's that?
GUARD TWO. Wind's up.
GUARD ONE. No, no. That sound—
GUARD TWO. Oh, that. They're interrogating the ghost of Hamlet's father.
GUARD ONE. Oh, I thought there was something wrong.
GUARD TWO. He's a tough one.
GUARD ONE. The ghost?
GUARD TWO. No. Eight Eyes. He's been crushing him for four solid hours.
GUARD ONE. Why doesn't the Ghost confess?
GUARD TWO. Maybe he hasn't got anything to confess. Give me a swig.
GUARD ONE. [*ignoring his request and having a drink himself*] Well, it's easy to confess when you *have* something to confess. I don't sympathize with him just because he's innocent. Why'd he volunteer for this Ghost mission in the first place? Too ambitious, that's his trouble. Wanted to get himself noticed. Don't like pushy people, myself.
GUARD TWO. He wasn't all that pushy. He was volunteered for the job by Eight Eyes. In fact, he tried to

refuse, said he was afraid of heights and he didn't like to work in the dark. Said his voice wasn't up to it.

[*Another howl is heard.*]

GUARD ONE. Voice sounds all right to me.

GUARD TWO. But they say Hamlet almost died from laughter when he saw him.

GUARD ONE. I heard Hamlet believed the whole thing. And how is our King?

GUARD TWO. [*lowering his voice*] He's been sick for some time now.

GUARD ONE. [*taking a swig*] No really?

GUARD TWO. Very sick. Didn't you see him on the national holiday?

GUARD ONE. Of course, I saw him. He was sitting on his throne.

GUARD TWO. Did you see him move?

GUARD ONE. Why would he move? If I were King, I wouldn't move.

GUARD TWO. Yeah, me neither.

GUARD ONE. Look what happened last time. He didn't move for two years and then suddenly he got up and strangled an ambassador. He doesn't move because everything's OK. If anything goes wrong, he'll move.

GUARD TWO. Give me a swig.

GUARD ONE. [*ignoring him, again*] How does it look? Are we going to invade Denmark again?

GUARD TWO. Who the fuck knows?

GUARD ONE. Do you think they'll fight back?

GUARD TWO. Who the fuck knows?

GUARD ONE. [*paranoia setting in*] Do you think someone is listening to us?

GUARD TWO. Who the fuck knows?

GUARD ONE. That's not good. I don't like talking if no one's listening. My thoughts get all confused.

GUARD TWO. Why shouldn't the Danes fight? They fought the first time we invaded them. [*growing nostalgic*] Oh, I was young then. When I think about the number of women I raped at their own request . . .

GUARD ONE. Yeah? Danish women?

GUARD TWO. Gimme a swig, will you?

GUARD ONE. [*handing over the bottle, looks anxiously as* GUARD TWO *takes a long swig. Finally,* GUARD ONE *grabs the bottle out of his hand.*] Hey, stop it!

GUARD TWO. One little piece tried to get out of it though. She told me, "I wouldn't do that if I were you. I've got the clap." I says to her, "Sweetie, you obviously don't know me!"

GUARD ONE. And did she have it?

GUARD TWO. [*indignant*] Of course, she did. Do you think I'm stupid?

GUARD ONE. At least, you had a chance to live it up a bit. Who do you think'll be the next King?

GUARD TWO. Mortinbras, of course.

GUARD ONE. What about Fortinbras?

GUARD TWO. Ah, he's younger and totally unreliable. People are saying that he stopped drinking.

GUARD ONE. No!

GUARD TWO. Yeah. It's why he's been recalled from the field.

[*The sound of trumpets offstage.* ANNOUNCER'S VOICE *from offstage*]

ANNOUNCER'S VOICE. Prince Fortinbras has arrived.

[*The* GUARDS *run out.*]

GUARD TWO. [*to* GUARD ONE] Hurry up. Get going.

Scene 4

[PRINCE MORTINBRAS, *Fortinbras's elder brother and successor to the throne of Norway, is sitting at his desk and writing. He looks like a typical intellectual from the beginning of the sixteenth century. Enter* FORTINBRAS *looking like a typical prince returning from a war.* MORTINBRAS *doesn't notice* FORTINBRAS's *entrance.*]

FORTINBRAS. [*clears his throat*] Ahem.

[MORTINBRAS *still doesn't notice* FORTINBRAS.]

FORTINBRAS. Brother.
MORTINBRAS. [*looks at him momentarily with moderate enthusiasm*] Oh, that's you, brother.

[MORTINBRAS *gets up and the two brothers embrace.*]

MORTINBRAS. Welcome home . . . You are not drunk.

[MORTINBRAS *immediately returns to his writing.*]

FORTINBRAS. [*passionately*] Of course not! You haven't heard that I quit?

[*During this conversation* FORTINBRAS *is removing his military attire. He throws down two extra swords, shin plates, heavy metal gloves, which hit the ground with a crash, breastplate, knee guards, etc. A very noisy untrussing.* MORTINBRAS *works unconcerned.*]

MORTINBRAS. [*never taking his eyes off his work*] I heard but I just didn't believe it.
FORTINBRAS. [*with typical ex-alcoholic enthusiasm*] Yeah.

I quit six weeks ago. I mean, the day after tomorrow it's going to be six weeks . . . day after tomorrow at four o'clock . . . A.M.

MORTINBRAS. [*still working feverishly*] It's a pity our
mother poisoned herself and didn't live to see this
day . . . How long do you think you can stay off?

FORTINBRAS. [*convinced completely*] This is it. I quit for
good this time.

MORTINBRAS. [*coldly*] Great. Then we'll have a chance
to talk. [*still working and not looking at him*] You
look much better.

FORTINBRAS. Actually when I was drinking I felt all
right. I mean physically, but it started to affect my
job. [*whispering*] You know, I burned the wrong
city. Fortunately it didn't get around because there
was a high wind and it went really fast but I felt
bad about it. I mean physically I felt all right but
psychologically . . .

MORTINBRAS. I know what you mean.

FORTINBRAS. Also I started to hallucinate.

MORTINBRAS. Hallucinate?

FORTINBRAS. You know, I saw things which . . . I'm
not sure.

MORTINBRAS. Interesting.

FORTINBRAS. Very interesting but my horse, that was
it.

MORTINBRAS. Your horse? What happened to your
horse?

FORTINBRAS. I hung him.

MORTINBRAS. Why?

FORTINBRAS. I thought he was somebody else.

MORTINBRAS. Who?

FORTINBRAS. I don't know. I was drunk.

MORTINBRAS. Uh huh.

FORTINBRAS. But I feel all right now. I mean psychologically but physically I'm fucked. These headaches, Jesus. . . . What are you writing?

MORTINBRAS. My friend Eight Eyes asked me to write him a short speech. Listen: "Fellow countrymen, once again we are united in sorrow and tragedy. A great man has been taken from us before his time. Let me assure you that the usual suspects are being rounded up for questioning and that the assassins will pay with their lives."

FORTINBRAS. Someone was killed?

MORTINBRAS. [*surprised*] No. Why?

[GUARDS *enter carrying food on platters. They set the plates down on the desk and exit.*]

FORTINBRAS. I'm hungry.

[FORTINBRAS *goes to stab a piece of meat with his knife.* MORTINBRAS *slaps his hand hard. The meat falls off.*]

MORTINBRAS. Wait! Are you crazy?

[MORTINBRAS *picks up one of* FORTINBRAS's *heavy metal gloves and flings it hard into a mound of animal skins which is lying off to one side of the stage.*]

FOODTASTER. [*from under the pile*] Ugh.

[*The girl* FOODTASTER *appears from under the mound, bundled up in rags. Her face is not visible. She scampers over to the table, takes food from every plate, and wolfs it down hungrily, using both hands.*]

MORTINBRAS. [*proudly*] She's my foodtaster.

FORTINBRAS. Are you afraid of being poisoned?

MORTINBRAS. No. Why? Give her some time.

[*The two of them stare at the* FOODTASTER *as she eats voraciously.*]

MORTINBRAS. She's a real find. Deaf, dumb, blind, can't read or write, no tastebuds but . . . I can't tell actually. I bribed the chief of tortures a fortune to fix her up for me.

FORTINBRAS. Poor thing.

[FORTINBRAS *tries to comfort the girl by patting her on the head. She bites his hand.*]

MORTINBRAS. She likes you.

[MORTINBRAS *checks the* FOODTASTER*'s eyes, looks up under her dress briefly, then punches her in the stomach. He seems satisfied.*]

MORTINBRAS. We can eat.

[*They start eating.*]

MORTINBRAS. My friend, Eight Eyes . . .

FORTINBRAS. I didn't know that Eight Eyes was a friend of yours.

MORTINBRAS. Of course! He's made a spectacular career here. He's a man on the way up.

FORTINBRAS. But the last time we talked about him you said he was a no-account assassin.

MORTINBRAS. Impossible. Maybe I said that he was a simple man and that he could have better manners. MAYBE! But I also happen to remember telling you that he never lost a duel.

FORTINBRAS. But you said that's because he dips his swords in poison first.

MORTINBRAS. [*furious and scared*] You're talking nonsense! You've been drunk for twenty years. You
don't know anything. I want you to know that the
greatest diplomat of our century and our father's
chief adviser, Sternborg, trusts Eight Eyes implicitly.

FORTINBRAS. OK. You're right. I was drunk but not
anymore. How is Daddy?

MORTINBRAS. Excellent.

FORTINBRAS. Did he happen to mention to you why he
recalled me?

MORTINBRAS. No, but I haven't spoken to him for
some time. For two years, to be exact. I mean, tomorrow it will be two years, at five.

FORTINBRAS. For two years? But why?

MORTINBRAS. He doesn't trust me.

FORTINBRAS. Why?

MORTINBRAS. Why, why. I don't know why. But
Sternborg and Eight Eyes are working on him for
me and any day now I expect everything to be
cleared up. Then father will invite me to dinner.

[*Fanfare.*]

VOICE OF ANNOUNCER. [*over loudspeaker*] Prince Mortinbras, Heir to the Throne, is hereby invited to
dinner with the King. I repeat Prince Mortinbras
. . .

[VOICE OF ANNOUNCER *becomes completely garbled, due
to technical difficulties.*]

MORTINBRAS. [*jumps for joy*] Aha! Didn't I tell you?
Eight Eyes. He did it for me. You see what it means
to have a true friend?

FORTINBRAS. Listen, when you see Father ask him why he recalled me, will you?

MORTINBRAS. [*changing his clothes*] I think I'll wear this one. No, this one.

FORTINBRAS. I'm afraid Father might want me to take the army back to Denmark. I don't want to do that again.

MORTINBRAS. They're still wearing these stockings in Denmark, aren't they? Father's fond of pastels. I'll wear these.

[*Enter* DAGNY BORG, *a flamboyantly dressed girl. She walks across the stage and disappears.* MORTINBRAS *doesn't notice her.* FORTINBRAS *follows the girl with his eyes.*]

FORTINBRAS. [*concerned*] Who was she?

MORTINBRAS. What?

FORTINBRAS. The girl.

MORTINBRAS. What girl?

[FORTINBRAS *points to where the girl was and rubs his eyes, uncertain about what he's seen.*]

MORTINBRAS. How do I look?

FORTINBRAS. Great. But Brother, wait a minute.

[MORTINBRAS *is exiting.*]

MORTINBRAS. Wait here. I'll be back.

DARKNESS

Scene 5

[*Enter* DAGNY BORG, *Sternborg's niece (the same girl who sashayed across the stage in the previous scene). She is followed by the* GUARDS, *who are struggling under the weight of her suitcases and boxes.* FORTINBRAS *watches her carefully, visibly relieved that she is not a hallucination. Just at that moment,* GUARD TWO *drops one of her heavier boxes and Dagny's books scatter all over the stage. She is very angry.*]

FORTINBRAS. [*looks at the books on the ground*] What are those?

[FORTINBRAS *and* GUARDS *exchange suspicious glances.* GUARDS *shrug.*]

DAGNY BORG. [*looks at him carefully*] They're books.
FORTINBRAS. Have you read all of these?

[FORTINBRAS *and* GUARDS *break up laughing over this idea.*]

DAGNY BORG. [*watching* FORTINBRAS *again*] Who are you?
FORTINBRAS. [*fighting down his laughter*] I'm Prince Fortinbras.
DAGNY BORG. Ah, Prince Fortinbras. So you're not drunk?
FORTINBRAS. [*proudly*] You heard about me? But I quit drinking six weeks ago.
DAGNY BORG. [*to* GUARDS] Hurry up with those books, assholes.

[GUARDS *start picking up the books and begin reloading them for* DAGNY.]

FORTINBRAS. I mean, the day after tomorrow it will be six weeks.

[FORTINBRAS *picks up one book and hands it to her.*]

DAGNY BORG. Thank you. Do you know Montaigne?

FORTINBRAS. [*wasn't sure he heard her correctly*] The French General?

[DAGNY BORG *starts laughing. The* GUARDS *join her.*]

FORTINBRAS. What's so funny?

[GUARDS *immediately stop laughing and shrug.*]

DAGNY BORG. [*still laughing*] It's a pity Hamlet isn't here. He'd enjoy this.

FORTINBRAS. The Prince, right?

DAGNY BORG. Right.

FORTINBRAS. So you know Hamlet?

DAGNY BORG. Everybody knows Hamlet.

FORTINBRAS. He must be the most famous Dane in the world. But where do you know him from?

DAGNY BORG. From Wittenberg.

[GUARDS *confirm this information by nodding their heads in agreement.*]

FORTINBRAS. From the university? What did you study? Theology?

[FORTINBRAS *winks at the* GUARDS. *They all break up into laughter, making copulation gestures suggestive of what* DAGNY *probably studied.*]

DAGNY BORG. It's nice to be home.

FORTINBRAS. [*tries to stop laughing*] Sorry. What's your name?

DAGNY BORG. Dagny Borg.

FORTINBRAS. Wait a minute. I heard about you when I was in Wittenberg.

DAGNY BORG. You've been in Wittenberg?

FORTINBRAS. Well, changing horses.

DAGNY BORG. [*to* GUARDS] Watch those bindings!

FORTINBRAS. Dagny Borg. Yes . . . now I remember. You had a love affair with Professor Luther.

DAGNY BORG. Typical university gossip.

FORTINBRAS. Then you ran away with that magician.

DAGNY BORG. [*indignantly*] I beg your pardon. Dr. Faustus is not a magician. He's an outstanding scholar.

FORTINBRAS. Then you got booed off the stage. So what brought you home again? There's no cultural exchange here.

DAGNY BORG. I was invited.

FORTINBRAS. By whom?

DAGNY BORG. Sternborg.

FORTINBRAS. Sternborg?

DAGNY BORG. Sternborg! I happen to be his niece.

[GUARDS *nod with respect toward* DAGNY.]

FORTINBRAS. You happen to be his niece?

DAGNY BORG. What's so strange about that?

FORTINBRAS. It's a little strange.

DAGNY BORG. I should go.

[DAGNY BORG *waves to the* GUARDS *to follow her.*]

FORTINBRAS. Wait. When am I going to see you again?

[DAGNY BORG *just leaves with the* GUARDS *and her belongings.*]

DARKNESS

Scene 6

[*King's tent from the outside. We hear the noises from inside the tent of a big dinner celebration: laughter, broken glasses, belching.*

Enter FORTINBRAS, *who comes over to the tent, stops by the entrance, then hesitates. He's afraid to enter without permission. He begins to look for an entrance so he can get inside (or at least see what's going on). Finding none he turns away. Then he makes a decision. He walks toward the tent and violently draws the entrance-flap back and winds up face to face with* EIGHT EYES *and* STERNBORG *(not whom he intended to run into). Inside the tent the throne can be seen, its back toward the audience. A crown rests somewhere in the vicinity of the king's head.*]

STERNBORG. Welcome, Prince. You can't imagine how very happy I am that you stopped drinking.
EIGHT EYES. Oh yes. We are all very happy for you.

[FORTINBRAS *tries to look inside the tent past* STERNBORG *and* EIGHT EYES, *but they block his path like a brick wall, moving where he moves.*]

FORTINBRAS. I'm very happy to see you too.
STERNBORG. [*as if nothing's going on*] Are you looking for something?
FORTINBRAS. You know my father recalled me so I came and . . .
STERNBORG. [*interrupting*] We know but he's very busy right now. He can't talk to you yet. He's in the middle of a dinner meeting with your brother.
FORTINBRAS. It'll take just a second. [*yells*] DADDY.
STERNBORG. We would love to help you, Prince, but

we are powerless. [*sign of resignation*] The King's
orders.

EIGHT EYES. The King of Finland is coming.

STERNBORG. The extension of trade credits is at stake.

EIGHT EYES. We are going to reduce the size of our
army as an exchange.

STERNBORG. To prove our peaceful intentions.

EIGHT EYES. The entire sixteenth regiment.

STERNBORG. An extremely risky decision.

EIGHT EYES. Very delicate.

FORTINBRAS. But maybe after dinner.

STERNBORG. It's going to be a very long dinner.

EIGHT EYES. Seventeen courses.

STERNBORG. And it's getting cold.

[*The two of them go back into the tent, closing the flap in*
FORTINBRAS*'s face.*]

DARKNESS

Scene 7

[*Enter the* GUARDS.]

GUARD ONE. What time is it?

GUARD TWO. Good idea. I wouldn't mind having a
drink myself.

[GUARD ONE *goes to the tree, pulls out a bottle of vodka
which was hidden in the trunk. He drinks and passes it to*
GUARD TWO, *who takes a swig and is paralyzed.*]

GUARD TWO. [*regaining his voice*] What's that?

GUARD ONE. [*proudly*] I added a bit of varnish. It keeps
your feet from sweating.

GUARD TWO. Gimme some more!

GUARD ONE. You know what would be nice? Some food.

GUARD TWO. [*nostalgically*] Yeah.

GUARD ONE. I heard that there's some coming from Finland.

GUARD TWO. No. Really?

GUARD ONE. Yes. As a reward for eliminating the sixteenth regiment . . .

GUARD TWO. You mean the five thousand naked soldiers who demanded clothes so Sternborg was forced to bury them alive?

GUARD ONE. Yeah. Those.

GUARD TWO. [*takes another swig*] Well, even if the Finns don't bring us the food, the King did personally guarantee our children will get some food or if not them then their children or their children's children or somebody.

GUARD ONE. He's a great king. [*smashes the empty bottle against the tree.*]

GUARD TWO. Not my children's children, unfortunately, because of the clap I caught in Denmark . . .

GUARD ONE. And which you gave to me! [GUARD ONE *trips over something, bends down and picks up* MORTINBRAS*'s neatly severed head, which he examines closely.*] Hey, look! It's Mortinbras.

GUARD TWO. Are you crazy? Mortinbras was much taller that that . . . [*indicates with his hand how much taller* MORTINBRAS *was.*] Get rid of it. [GUARD ONE *tosses the head to* GUARD TWO, *who involuntarily catches it.*]

GUARD TWO. Don't throw it to me, you shit.

[GUARD TWO *tosses the head back to* GUARD ONE. GUARD ONE *tosses it back again. They both run toward the exit, tossing the head back and forth, using some tricks from American professional baseball.*]

DARKNESS

Scene 8

[*As* FORTINBRAS *enters, the head of* MORTINBRAS *comes flying across the stage.* FORTINBRAS *catches it as if by instinct.*

After a second he recognizes his brother's head.]

FORTINBRAS. Oh Brother.

[*Suddenly* FORTINBRAS *is stricken with a violent migraine. He puts* MORTINBRAS*'s head on the ground and grabs his own head in pain.*

FORTINBRAS *then notices the bottle left onstage by the* GUARDS. *He picks it up and drinks hungrily, for a long time, until it is completely drained. Then he tosses the empty behind him. The pain is gone and he feels visibly better.*

Once again he picks up MORTINBRAS*'s head and cradles it in his arm.*]

FORTINBRAS. Alas, poor Mortinbras.

[*Behind* FORTINBRAS, *the* GHOST OF HIS FATHER *appears, a very poorly dressed former man between sixty and eighty.*]

GHOST. Get rid of that. Carrying around a severed head after sunset brings bad luck.

[FORTINBRAS *drops the head, pulls out his sword, and turns to the* GHOST. *As soon as he sees who it is,* FORTINBRAS *goes limp and gives up his fighting stance in resignation.*]

FORTINBRAS. No. Not you again.

GHOST. You don't know how it warms my heart to see you drinking again. Listen, Son, God protects only rapists, drunkards, and little children. To be sober is to spit in his eye. Help him to take care of you. Drink! Then we can talk.

FORTINBRAS. Get out of here.

GHOST. It's not very nice to talk like that to your father's ghost. [*giggling*] Maybe you'd like to try and chop off my head again. Go on. I don't mind.

[FORTINBRAS *makes the sign of the cross over the* GHOST.]

GHOST. Don't behave like an idiot. Funny, Hamlet believed in a fake ghost immediately and you don't want to believe in a real one. That's what comes of a secular education.

FORTINBRAS. You can't be my father. My father is alive. I saw him today. [*he points at the head*] He's having dinner with my brother, Mortinbras, right now. And. . . .

[FORTINBRAS *catches his mistake*]

GHOST. [*giggles*] That's right. Maybe it's getting through to you now. I already told you, you idiot, I was killed exactly two years ago. In July. At the end of July. The 24th of July, to be exact, before dinner.

FORTINBRAS. [*shocked*] Before dinner?

GHOST. Don't repeat it. I'm not deaf.

FORTINBRAS. But . . . who killed you?

GHOST. Sternborg, of course. He's wiping out our entire dynasty.

FORTINBRAS. [*incensed*] The murderer.

GHOST. Well, that's beside the point. [*distracted*] Don't interrupt me. I hate it! So, where were we? Oh, so he killed me. It's unfortunate but it happens. What really pisses me off is what happened after he killed me.

FORTINBRAS. After he killed you?

GHOST. [*hits him on the head*] Don't repeat it! He left me sitting there on the throne like a prop. I'm not a prop. I mean this is confusing. The Norwegian empire is being run by a butcher who's using my name and ruining my reputation.

FORTINBRAS. Listen.

GHOST. I know what you want to say. Granted. I was ruthless but don't compare me with Sternborg. Whatever I did was done very close to the rules of civilized behavior.

FORTINBRAS. Father.

GHOST. At last, my son.

[GHOST *opens his arms wide. They embrace.*]

FORTINBRAS. Do you know where I can get some more vodka?

[GHOST *leads* FORTINBRAS, *still clutched in an embrace, over to the hollow of the tree, reaches in and pulls out another bottle of vodka left by the* GUARDS. GHOST *hands the bottle to* FORTINBRAS. FORTINBRAS *drinks.*]

GHOST. Son, between the two of us, you knew perfectly well that I'd been dead for the past two years.

FORTINBRAS. No I didn't.

GHOST. Yes you did. So don't treat me like a nightmare. I'm real.

FORTINBRAS. I can't see you in the mirror.

GHOST. I know. It's embarrassing. It's not because I'm
vain. It's because I've always been a materialist and
don't think I've stopped being one just because I
became a ghost. Understand? I mean look at me.
Don't look at my clothes. I had to steal them.
Look at me, dialectically. Listen, in order to grasp
who one is, one has to grasp who one isn't, right?
It seems as though what one is comes about only
in opposition to what one isn't. And vice versa, of
course. Can't you stop shivering?

FORTINBRAS. I'm cold.

[FORTINBRAS *begins to get more and more agitated, pacing
around the stage as if he's looking for something.*]

GHOST. Look, if one is a ghost or a walking proof of
the fallacy of materialism, that is, being immate-
rial, then from this premise it follows that matter
exists. Therefore, we can reasonably deduce that
matter is the condition without which ghosts cannot exist. That's the reason I consented to become
a ghost in the first place.

[GHOST *starts to shiver.*]

FORTINBRAS. Are you cold?

[FORTINBRAS *has made up his mind. He begins a deliber-
ate hunt for all his discarded military attire . . . his heavy
metal gloves, shinplates, kneepads, breastplates, etc.*]

GHOST. And hot too! I'm a mass of contradictions.
Theoretically, it's amusing, but living like this is

difficult. Even if, as in my case, one isn't actually living, it's still difficult. [GHOST *notices* FORTIN- BRAS*'s activity*] What the hell do you think you're doing?

FORTINBRAS. I'm leaving.

GHOST. No you're not.

[FORTINBRAS *grabs all his equipment, ready to depart.*]

FORTINBRAS. I've got to run away. I'm going to be next.

[GHOST *tries to grab the equipment out of* FORTINBRAS*'s arms. They struggle.*]

FORTINBRAS. Get out of my way.

GHOST. Don't you think you have something to do here?

FORTINBRAS. Leave me alone.

[GHOST *grabs* FORTINBRAS *and the two of them wrestle to the ground. First one and then the other has the advantage.*]

GHOST. [*as they fight fiercely*] Bury me, you son of a bitch.

FORTINBRAS. [*an early physical advantage*] Now?

GHOST. Now.

FORTINBRAS. [*strangling the ghost*] Sternborg will never agree to it.

GHOST. [*gasping for wind*] Then you'll have to bury him first.

FORTINBRAS. He won't agree to that either.

GHOST. [*the struggle continues where the* GHOST *has a real advantage, sitting on top of* FORTINBRAS *and strangling him*] How far do you think you'd get without the aid of your family?

[FORTINBRAS *is gagging incoherently.*]

GHOST. Don't you remember that you were always my favorite. I used to ride you on my horse when you were a little boy.

FORTINBRAS. [*gasps for breath; makes inarticulate sounds like*] strangling . . . me . . . [*gasps.*]

GHOST. [*lets up a bit*] Sorry, Son. Where were you going to run, you fool?

FORTINBRAS. [*still gasping for breath*] My army . . . my camp . . . my soldiers are faithful to me.

GHOST. [*laughs cruelly*] Ha ha.

FORTINBRAS. Then to Finland.

GHOST. You will never get past the border.

FORTINBRAS. Denmark then.

GHOST. King Claudius is Sternborg's agent. He'd hand you over before you'd ever reached the guerillas. Besides, you know they haven't got a chance even if Hamlet decided to lead them. You have no place to run. Nobody ever escaped from Norway, you idiot.

FORTINBRAS. So what should I do?

GHOST. Look. Sternborg is not expecting a move from you yet. You can catch him by surprise if you murder him tonight. I personally recommend poison in the ear. He'll listen to that. After [*makes a throat slitting move*] Eight Eyes, then declare yourself King and bury me.

FORTINBRAS. OK, but look, Daddy . . .

VOICE OF ANNOUNCER. Prince Fortinbras is hereby in-

vited to dinner with the King. I repeat Prince Fortinbras . . .

[VOICE OF ANNOUNCER *becomes completely garbled due to
technical difficulties.* GHOST *gets off* FORTINBRAS *and
dusts himself off in disgust.*]

GHOST. Shit!
FORTINBRAS. So what should I do?
GHOST. [*disgusted*] It's too late. Forget it. Finito.

[GHOST *is preparing to leave.* FORTINBRAS *grabs him by his
gown.*]

FORTINBRAS. There's no chance?
GHOST. You have only one chance, that after they kill
      you they'll bury you.
FORTINBRAS. [*calling after him*] Daddy. Daddy. Wait!

[GHOST *exits.* FORTINBRAS *goes over to the tree, takes out
another bottle of vodka, and drinks the whole thing down.*]

DARKNESS

[*We hear the sounds of* FORTINBRAS *drinking, breathing
out, and drinking some more.*]

Scene 9

[*Sternborg's tent.* EIGHT EYES *enters. He takes a look
around the stage, pulls out his rapier, and makes a couple of
thrusts through the curtain around the stage. A scream is
heard offstage and the noise of a falling body.*]

EIGHT EYES. Oh shit. I forgot I asked the barber to
      wait. I knew I forgot about something. [*shrugs*]

[*From one side of the stage,* TWO GUARDS *carry out the*

*King's throne with the dead King seated on it. They leave
the throne and exit. A few moments later, they reenter carrying a barrel of water with* STERNBORG *seated inside,
ready for his bath. They add some more hot water to the
tub, bow to* STERNBORG, *and disappear.*]

STERNBORG. [*splashing water over himself*] I must say,
civilization has its good points. [*grunts delightedly*]
Did Fortinbras get the invitation?

EIGHT EYES. Yes he did. [*hands* STERNBORG *a cake of
soap*]

STERNBORG. [*lathering up*] A most satisfactory night.
Any problems?

EIGHT EYES. The Finns have found out that one of our
armies is moving on the Danish border . . .

STERNBORG. And they're screaming again?

EIGHT EYES. Yes, they're saying that all treaties seem to
end where Norway begins.

STERNBORG. They're right.

EIGHT EYES. They've got a big army.

STERNBORG. We've got a bigger one.

EIGHT EYES. But not as well equipped.

STERNBORG. What are we short of mainly?

EIGHT EYES. Well, mainly breastplates, chain mail, helmets, hatchets, arrows, oh yes, and swords.

STERNBORG. What about shields?

EIGHT EYES. And shields . . . and shoes too.

STERNBORG. Don't worry. The Finns aren't going to
start a war over a puny little country like Denmark.
God, I'm so sick of this. Of course, they can invade
any principality anytime they wish but whenever
we crush Denmark they shriek. But as long as they
don't cancel our historical meeting we're all right.

EIGHT EYES. Right.

STERNBORG. Has Polonius arrived yet?

EIGHT EYES. I will check.

[EIGHT EYES *exits.*]

[STERNBORG, *still immersed in the barrel, whistles a tune.*
POLONIUS *enters, a well-dressed man who is quite frightened.* STERNBORG *stands in the barrel, opens his wet arms
to greet him.*]

STERNBORG. Hail, Polonius. [*hugs* POLONIUS, *leaving
him dripping wet*]

POLONIUS. [*begins speaking in an unsure tone of voice. He
addresses neither* STERNBORG *nor the King directly*] I
greet you in the name of the Danish people who
send you through me their expression of brotherly
love. The whole Danish nation, from infant to old
man, knows how much we owe to the Norwegian
people . . . [POLONIUS *looks attentively at the King,
breaks off for a second, then asks* STERNBORG *more
quietly*] And how is the King, the greatest friend of
Danish children.

STERNBORG. Very well. Very well. He was so happy
when he heard you were coming. You know how
he loves the Danes.

POLONIUS. We know. We know.

STERNBORG. I won't hide the fact that here in Norway
not everybody loves you as much as he does. But
while he's alive you have nothing to fear.

POLONIUS. [*studying the King at length*] Yes, indeed, he
looks . . . very well. Because you know, when I
saw him last time, he struck me as looking a bit

pale. Am I mistaken or has His Majesty moved his hand a little bit since the last time I saw him?

STERNBORG. Which one?

POLONIUS. The left one, but on the other hand, if you take it from His Majesty's point of view, the right one.

STERNBORG. Do you think so?

POLONIUS. The left one. The ring finger last time was parallel to the orb or from His Majesty's point of view to the scepter. On the other hand . . .

STERNBORG. [*interrupting*] Sit down, my friend. Sit down. [*indicates a place, but there is nothing to sit on but the ground.*]

POLONIUS. [*looking around, helplessly*] No thank you. I'd rather stretch my legs.

STERNBORG. So, what's going on in Denmark?

POLONIUS. Well, you know how people are. Grumble, grumble . . .

STERNBORG. [*threatening*] About what?

POLONIUS. Oh you know, the unpopular measures: murder on the throne, occupation . . .

STERNBORG. What occupation?

POLONIUS. You know, your army either standing on the border or actually marching across the country and then the usual stories of how you are robbing us of everything and then there is always misery, lawlessness, hunger.

[GUARDS *enter carrying a groaning board of fancy feast foods. They walk it past* POLONIUS *who is obviously hungry.* POLONIUS *wipes his lips as he continues to talk to* STERNBORG. *The* GUARDS *set up the table and a few chairs and then exit.*]

POLONIUS. [*licking his chops*] No pleasing some people. But it's a small faction. Ten, maybe eleven million. No more.

STERNBORG. Will you please soap my back?

POLONIUS. With pleasure. [*soaps* STERNBORG's *back*]

STERNBORG. You discussed their attitudes with them?

POLONIUS. Naturally. For their own good, to protect them from the wrath of the Danish people, we gathered them up in one place.

STERNBORG. Where?

POLONIUS. We dug some holes in the ground. They're called "The Pits of the King." The hostile elements have been interred there under excellent conditions.

STERNBORG. And are they still complaining?

POLONIUS. To tell the truth, there's been some snowfall and since then we can't make them out too clearly.

STERNBORG. Good. And does the general public approve?

POLONIUS. Oh, ecstatically. One hundred percent behind us on the King's Pit business and gratitude for your army's successful occupation.

STERNBORG. Rinse it! [*points to his back.*]

POLONIUS. [*doing it without question*] Love to.

STERNBORG. [*lowering his voice*] In other words, they hate us.

POLONIUS. [*lowering his voice*] If they could, they'd hate us.

STERNBORG. I expected that, but it still wounds me to hear it.

POLONIUS. Unfortunately, the King's Pits have stirred up the guerillas again.

STERNBORG. [*threatening*] Guerillas?

[STERNBORG *emerges from the bath.* POLONIUS *helps him
get dry, wraps towels around him.* STERNBORG *claps his
hands. Enter the* GUARDS. POLONIUS *gets visibly alarmed,
but as it turns out, quite needlessly.*]

STERNBORG. [*to the* GUARDS] His Majesty wishes to take
a nap.

[*The* GUARDS *start to carry out the throne with the dead
King on it.* POLONIUS *bows ceremoniously to the King,
starts to say something gracious, but then gives it up as a
futile gesture. The King is carried out.* STERNBORG *gets
dressed with* POLONIUS's *help.*]

STERNBORG. And what about the relations between
Hamlet and King Claudius?

POLONIUS. Hard to say. Seems OK, but they could be
better. All considered, I'd say they're awful. On
the other hand, I could be wrong since Prince
Hamlet tends to express himself metaphorically
. . .

STERNBORG. Metaphorically?

POLONIUS. Even hypermetaphorically.

STERNBORG. I think I understand.

POLONIUS. I don't.

STERNBORG. Did Hamlet go to that secret meeting
with the guerilla leaders?

POLONIUS. He did.

STERNBORG. [*threatening*] Did he?

POLONIUS. [*hastily*] Oh yes. He went, but he didn't get
there.

STERNBORG. What do you mean?

POLONIUS. I mean, he got dressed, put on a mask, left

Elsinore, and once outside the castle, stopped to reflect, came back inside, got undressed, and lay down on the bed . . .

STERNBORG. [*relieved*] I see.

POLONIUS. But then he got dressed again, put the mask on, and got undressed again. And then . . .

STERNBORG. [*interrupting*] Got dressed again?

POLONIUS. That's right. How did you know? And he talks to himself all the time. On the other hand, I am happy to report relations between the Prince and his mother have taken a turn for the better. They're really on very good terms now.

STERNBORG. Very good?

POLONIUS. Maybe even better than very good.

STERNBORG. Aha . . . I see what you mean.

POLONIUS. I think it's why King Claudius has been complaining of insomnia lately.

STERNBORG. Interesting . . . Tell me, does Hamlet ever mention his late father?

POLONIUS. Not a word. He used to talk about him all the time but now . . . [*he waves his hands as if to express his disapproval*]

STERNBORG. [*visibly pleased*] I see.

POLONIUS. You do? Young people nowadays . . . I don't want to boast, but my son, Laertes, is a real exception.

STERNBORG. Is he?

POLONIUS. He is.

[*Enter* EIGHT EYES.]

POLONIUS. [*enthusiastically*] Hail, Eight Eyes.

[EIGHT EYES *pays no attention to* POLONIUS.]

EIGHT EYES. Everything's ready.
POLONIUS. [*almost as enthusiastically as before*] Hail,
    Eight Eyes.
EIGHT EYES. [*icily*] Hi.

[*Enter* FORTINBRAS, *lurching. He's very drunk. Everyone
turns and stares at him, slightly shocked.* FORTINBRAS *stops
and wavers on his feet. He is holding a half-empty bottle of
vodka. He's staring into people's faces without really seeing
them.* STERNBORG *and* EIGHT EYES *exchange surprised
glances.*]

STERNBORG. [*after a moment of silence*] Good evening,
    Prince.

[FORTINBRAS *looks at him, desperately trying to recognize
him. Then suddenly his face lights up.*]

FORTINBRAS. Aha, Sternborg. My friend.

[FORTINBRAS *opens his arms, lurches toward* STERNBORG,
and kisses him passionately. STERNBORG *unenthusiasti-
cally accepts his greeting. With relief he sees that* FORTIN-
BRAS *has now noticed* EIGHT EYES.]

FORTINBRAS. [*uncertainly*] Eight Eyes?
EIGHT EYES. Yes, Prince.

[FORTINBRAS *grabs* EIGHT EYES *and gives him a passionate kiss and double-armed bear hug, hammering his back
robustly. While still embracing and mauling* EIGHT EYES,
FORTINBRAS *notices* POLONIUS, *who is standing modestly
off to one side.*]

FORTINBRAS. [*of* POLONIUS'*s sour expression*] Who's that
    Great Dane over there?

[POLONIUS *smiles and bows.*]

STERNBORG. It's King Claudius's minister, Polonius.
FORTINBRAS. Woof woof. [*he laughs*]

[FORTINBRAS *still hangs onto* EIGHT EYES, *swaying.*]

FORTINBRAS. So it's you, you dog-faced piece of shit.

[FORTINBRAS *abandons* EIGHT EYES *and goes for* POLO-
NIUS. *He claps* POLONIUS *on the stomach, takes a drink
from his bottle, and passes it to* POLONIUS.]

FORTINBRAS. Lap it up, you miserable hound.
POLONIUS. [*with polite dignity*] No thank you, Prince.
FORTINBRAS. Drink, it's good for you, Pig Face. I love
    you, you old Danish ass-kisser. You old kiss-ass
    Dane.
POLONIUS. That's very sweet of you, Prince, but no.
FORTINBRAS. [*offended*] No?
POLONIUS. No.
FORTINBRAS. You are not going to drink with Fortin-
    bras, Prince of the fucking realm?
POLONIUS. But please, Prince. Let's eat first.
FORTINBRAS. [*angry*] Shut up! You scorn me, huh? You
    think I'm not educated. And you're right. I'm not
    educated. [*full of self-pity*] I'm just a simple fucking
    soldier but I love you, you pig-faced old bastard.
    And I love my country, my mother Norway, which
    is watching me making a fucking ass of myself, try-
    ing to get you to take a goddamned drink. [*he weeps
    heartily*] Motherfucking Norway.
STERNBORG. Prince, food.
FORTINBRAS. [*halts them from eating*] Wait. I'm not
    done with him.

[FORTINBRAS *grabs* POLONIUS *by the collar.*]

FORTINBRAS. You drinking or not?
POLONIUS. [*convinced*] By all means, Prince.

[POLONIUS *takes a big swig, coughs violently.* STERNBORG *and* EIGHT EYES *take their seats and start eating.*]

FORTINBRAS. Ah, my dog-faced friend. So, kiss me and forgive me because I'm a good fucking man. I am. And I love you. You know what? You remind me of my dog and God I loved that dog. He was a little bit shorter than you but he was the one fucking person in the world that I really loved. And he loved me too. Then one day, when I took him for a walk . . .

[*He begins weeping.* FORTINBRAS *embraces* POLONIUS *and gives him a long kiss on the mouth, after which they both wipe their lips and spit on the ground.*]

FORTINBRAS. Let's eat.

[FORTINBRAS *and* POLONIUS *join* EIGHT EYES *and* STERNBORG *at dinner.*]

STERNBORG. [*toasts*] To the tradition of friendship between Denmark and Norway.

[*They all toast.*]

FORTINBRAS. Listen, all of you. Maybe you want to know why I'm drinking, huh? Aha. Well, you can tear the skin off my back but I'm not going to tell you. [FORTINBRAS *gets to his feet. To* POLONIUS] Are you listening, you pigfucker? Look, now I'm telling you. Listen I'm drinking because . . .

[FORTINBRAS *collapses unconscious on the table.*]

POLONIUS. I don't know what to think about this.

STERNBORG. Whatever you want, Polonius. Whatever you want.

POLONIUS. [*toasts*] To Danish Norwegian friendship . . .

[STERNBORG *claps his hands suddenly, making* POLONIUS *jump and spill his drink. But the clap was only a signal for the singing to begin offstage. It's a plaintive Norwegian tune, something along the lines of the "Song of the Volga Boatman." All present join in the singing. At a certain moment* STERNBORG *raises his finger and the singing comes to an abrupt halt.*]

POLONIUS. [*extremely moved*] I love this modern music.

STERNBORG. I'm glad that a connoisseur like yourself appreciates our art.

POLONIUS. All the artists and greatest minds in Denmark know how much they owe to me and I know how to talk to them. Poor Yorick used to dine with me. I myself, as you know, played Caesar at the Capitol. It was I who invited the actors to King Claudius's court. It was due to my personal intervention that Elsinore was the site of the world premiere of "The Murder of Gonzago."

EIGHT EYES. Why did you produce it?

POLONIUS. [*passionately*] Because I intended to prove, and I succeeded in doing so, that during times of intensified military buildup and police vigilance, art can and must flourish.

[FORTINBRAS *suddenly wakes up, whips out a dagger, and searches the scene with unseeing eyes for a villain to stab.*

EIGHT EYES *taps his arm with understanding.* FORTIN-
BRAS *sheaths his dagger and falls back to sleep.*]

STERNBORG. And how was the play received?
POLONIUS. It was a momentous triumph. It proved
    to the entire world that creative freedom in Den-
    mark was not a joke. Naturally, the public couldn't
    see the play because of the curfew but King Clau-
    dius was so moved by it that he had a heart attack
    and had to be carried out of the theater before the
    end of the first act. My wife and I enjoyed it im-
    mensely. Of course, our home has had a long-
    standing tradition of culture. Our daughter,
    Ophelia, acted on the stage before she started
    working for the police.

[FORTINBRAS *stands unsteadily. Everyone looks at him ex-
pectantly.*]

FORTINBRAS. I'm going to puke. [FORTINBRAS *takes a
    couple of steps. Everyone follows his movements with
    their eyes. They all rise and sway with him as if they're
    going to catch him if he falls.* FORTINBRAS *steadies
    himself, holds up his hand to show he's all right, takes
    one more step, and crashes heavily to the floor.*]
STERNBORG. I have to tell you, Polonius, that we here
    in Norway are a little bit disappointed in how King
    Claudius has handled the guerillas.
POLONIUS. But what about "The Pits of the King"?
STERNBORG. Spectacular but hollow. Our King would
    like to see you in Claudius's place.
POLONIUS. [*uncertainly*] But King Claudius is still
    alive.
STERNBORG. The line between life and death, my dear

Polonius, is incredibly fluid. Do you love King
Claudius?

POLONIUS. He has many achievements to his credit.
[*timidly*] Pits?

STERNBORG. He's a murderer. He has blood on his
hands.

POLONIUS. [*firmly*] That's right.

STERNBORG. On the other hand . . .

POLONIUS. Absolutely.

STERNBORG. I haven't said anything yet.

POLONIUS. I quite agree.

STERNBORG. OK, Polonius. Go back to Denmark and
wait.

POLONIUS. Absolutely.

[POLONIUS *gets up, looks around as if to ask permission to
leave. But no one's paying any attention to him.*]

POLONIUS. So, should I leave now? [*There's no reaction
from* STERNBORG *or* EIGHT EYES.]

POLONIUS. So maybe it would be better if I left now.

[*Still no reaction.* POLONIUS *bows and scrapes a few times
and then exits.*]

Scene 10

[FORTINBRAS *is lying on the floor drunk.* STERNBORG *and*
EIGHT EYES *talk.*]

STERNBORG. Amazing. Hamlet actually believed that
King Claudius killed his father. Great. He won't
want to lead the guerillas. I'll make you a bet: in
two weeks Hamlet kills Claudius. Bet?

EIGHT EYES. [*extends his hand. They shake.*] Bet. And

then we'll finish off Hamlet and put Polonius on
the throne.

STERNBORG. Polonius? No way. The people in Denmark hate him almost as much as Claudius. What
about his son, Laertes?

EIGHT EYES. A promising swordsman and a complete
idiot.

STERNBORG. Sounds good. Didn't Polonius say Laertes loves him?

EIGHT EYES. Absolutely.

STERNBORG. So, we'll give Laertes a chance to prove it.
What about knifing Polonius through a curtain
and making it look like Hamlet did it?

EIGHT EYES. Hamlet?

STERNBORG. Naturally. [*enumerating on his fingers*]
Then Hamlet will kill Claudius. Laertes will kill
Hamlet. Then Laertes will marry Hamlet's
mother, become king, and eliminate the guerillas.
So send someone to stab Polonius and get a letter
of condolence ready for Laertes, but don't do it
the way you did last time when the sympathy card
to Hamlet's mother arrived a week before we killed
her husband. [STERNBORG *points to* FORTINBRAS.]
Now let's get rid of that.

[EIGHT EYES *draws his sword, stands over* FORTINBRAS's
*drunken body, raises the weapon with both hands. At that
moment, there's a loud explosion offstage.*]

EIGHT EYES. [*thrown off balance, turns toward the sound*]
What's that?

STERNBORG. Oh shit. Not another attempt on the
king's life.

EIGHT EYES. Let's hope that this time he comes out of it in one piece.

[EIGHT EYES *again raises his sword to slay* FORTINBRAS. STERNBORG *stops him.*]

STERNBORG. Wait. Wait. Listen.

[*Both listen for the announcement.*]

VOICE OF ANNOUNCER. As a result of the attempted assassination, the King has lost the following: three fingers on his right hand, the index finger, the ring finger and the thumb . . .

STERNBORG. [*relieved*] It could have been much worse.

ANNOUNCER. . . . The right leg up to the knee . . .

STERNBORG. It can be sewn on.

ANNOUNCER. . . . The left leg up to the groin. The left hand to the elbow . . .

EIGHT EYES. Seems the left side took the worst beating . . .

ANNOUNCER. . . . The left ear . . .

EIGHT EYES. [*triumphantly*] That's what I was saying.

STERNBORG. Shut up.

ANNOUNCER. . . . The left ear, the entire nose . . . the left side of the face, the left eye . . .

STERNBORG. [*yells*] Enough. Stop it. Bring His Majesty in. Gently.

[*The* GUARDS *bring in the enthroned King or what's left of him. Pretty disgusting.* EIGHT EYES *gives a low whistle of admiration.*]

STERNBORG. Oh no.

ANNOUNCER. His Majesty, the King of Finland and the Finnish delegation have just arrived.

STERNBORG. Turn His Majesty so his right side is facing forward.

[*The* GUARDS *turn the throne.* STERNBORG *adjusts the crown on the King's multilated head.*]

EIGHT EYES. Didn't I tell you the left side took the worst of it?
STERNBORG. Shut up!

[STERNBORG *and* EIGHT EYES *flank the throne ceremoniously.* STERNBORG *makes the sign of the cross.* EIGHT EYES *points to* FORTINBRAS *with his sword.*]

EIGHT EYES. What about this?
STERNBORG. Not now.

DARKNESS

Scene 11

[*Enter the Finnish delegation consisting of two elegantly dressed officials. The Finnish delegates look at the King of Norway and exchange glances among themselves. Then they bow deeply in his direction.* STERNBORG *and* EIGHT EYES *respond with ceremonial bows. After a long silence . . .*]

STERNBORG. Are we not to be honored by the presence of the great King of Finland on this historic occasion?
FINN ONE. Oh damn. We left him in the cart.
FINN TWO. It'll just take a second.

[*The two* FINNS *scurry out to fetch the King. After a moment the screeching of wheels is heard. They return pushing*

*before them the sixteenth-century equivalent of a wheel-
chair. Sitting in it is a totally senile wisp of an old man.
His hair has been painted jet black (despite his advanced
age), and an imbecile's toothless grin creeps over his face
from time to time.* STERNBORG *and* EIGHT EYES *bow to this
new relic very seriously.*]

STERNBORG. A truly momentous occasion.
FINN ONE. History is being made before our very eyes.
EIGHT EYES. How fortunate I am to have lived to see
    this day.
FINN TWO. The responsibility for the entire human
    race rests upon their able shoulders.
STERNBORG. Let us leave them to their weighty delib-
    erations while we get some dinner.

[*All those present, except* FORTINBRAS, *who's lying in the
corner unconscious, bow to the Kings and leave, walking
backward. One of them inadvertently trips over the crum-
pled body of* FORTINBRAS, *without waking him. They pay
no attention to him and exit. The* KING OF FINLAND *smiles
amicably at the* KING OF NORWAY, *raises his hand with
some difficulty, and with still greater effort and after a
great inner struggle manages to utter.*]

FINNISH KING. Have a nice day.

DARKNESS

Scene 12

[*Same place.* STERNBORG *and* EIGHT EYES, *in a gloomy
mood, are sipping vodka from a bottle. The throne with the
remains of the* KING OF NORWAY *is standing nearby.
    During the conversation,* FORTINBRAS *staggers to his*

feet, extremely hung over, pays no attention to STERNBORG *or* EIGHT EYES *(and vice versa) but is only interested in finding more vodka. He empties all the bottles he can find while lurching around.* STERNBORG *and* EIGHT EYES *pay no attention to him either.*]

STERNBORG. [*grimly*] What a day we're having.

EIGHT EYES. I thought it went pretty well.

[*A piece of the* KING OF NORWAY *falls noisily to the floor.*]

STERNBORG. Hey, give us a break. [*looks gloomily at* EIGHT EYES] This is disgusting. No. A King like that is a disgrace to the throne. The King of Finland at least says three words.

EIGHT EYES. [*counts on his fingers*] "Have a nice day." Four.

STERNBORG. The crown won't even stay on His Majesty's head.

[STERNBORG *takes the crown off the mutilated head of the King and turns it in his hand.*]

EIGHT EYES. Why don't you try it?

[STERNBORG *tries on the crown. It's all gory. He wipes it on* EIGHT EYES*'s garment and then puts it back on his own head.*]

EIGHT EYES. It fits.

STERNBORG. [*takes it off*] Well, when I'm ready to die I'll put it on.

[*Just then* FORTINBRAS *lurches by in his search for alcohol, taking* STERNBORG*'s bottle out of his hand as he goes, as if neither* EIGHT EYES *nor* STERNBORG *were alive.* STERNBORG *and* EIGHT EYES *watch him now for the first* *time with some interest.* STERNBORG *still holds the crown in his hand.*]

STERNBORG. I must say, Fortinbras won me over today.

EIGHT EYES. I really enjoyed his company.

STERNBORG. All this intrigue that he'd quit drinking. [*shaking his head*] Oh people people. [*spinning the crown from one finger to the other*] What if we did something really daring . . . like burying that [*pointing at the* KING OF NORWAY] and placing that [*the crown he's still playing with*] on him. [*pointing to* FORTINBRAS]

EIGHT EYES. You mean kill him first and then . . . ?

STERNBORG. No! Just imagine. A live king . . .

EIGHT EYES. [*astounded*] Aha!

STERNBORG. Think of the admiration we'd get from the Liberals.

EIGHT EYES. [*taken with the idea*] Aha! Aha!

STERNBORG. But what if he sobers up? Yeah, that could be a problem. He could figure out that I killed his father and brother.

EIGHT EYES. So what?

STERNBORG. Well, how would you feel if you found out I killed your father and brother?

EIGHT EYES. But you did kill my father and brother. Did I ever say a word? Did I ever complain?

STERNBORG. No. You're right. Still, we'll have to keep an eye on him. Let's have a test. Dry him out a little.

[EIGHT EYES *tosses a bucket of water at* FORTINBRAS.]

DARKNESS

Scene 13

[*In the center of the stage is a bed covered with animal skins. Fanfares are heard. The royal court assembles.*]

STERNBORG. [*to* EIGHT EYES *about* FORTINBRAS] Remember. Don't take your eyes off him for a moment.

EIGHT EYES. I'm so excited.

FORTINBRAS. [*a little drunk but very excited*] I'm so excited. I should have a drink. I'm finally going to get to see her act. You know, I've never been in a theater before.

STERNBORG. Really, Prince? Neither have I.

FORTINBRAS. What sort of costume will she be in? Is she going to dance? Something vile maybe? I'm so excited.

STERNBORG. I'm so excited.

EIGHT EYES. I'm so excited.

[*Sound of trumpets offstage announce the beginning of the performance. The* KING'*s head is seen emerging from under a bedcover. The actor playing the role wears an exact replica of* FORTINBRAS'*s father's head. He puts his hands under the cover and pulls out the crown and places it on his head, puts his hand back again and this time pulls out a map and unfolds it on the bed.*]

FORTINBRAS. [*amused*] Hey, he looks just like my Dad!

STERNBORG. [*exchanging glances with* EIGHT EYES] Yes, there's a certain resemblance.

EIGHT EYES. Around the eyes.

[*Actor playing the role of* STERNBORG *bows several times.*]

FORTINBRAS. [*to* STERNBORG, *cheerfully*] Hey. He looks just like you!

STERNBORG. You think so, Prince?

EIGHT EYES. In the shoulders.

[*THE PLAY WITHIN THE PLAY: The actor playing the role of the* KING *greets the actor-*STERNBORG *amiably and hands the map to him. The actor-*STERNBORG *unfolds it. It's the Norwegian Empire, covering Scandinavia, eastern Europe, and extending to Asia. Using his index finger, the* KING *draws a line indicating the plans for future expansion of the territories. The actor-*STERNBORG *nods his approval with a big grin. They are just discussing the fate of Spain and perhaps France (or maybe even North and South America, possibly Africa and the Antarctic), when* DAGNY BORG *violently appears carrying two glasses of wine. They toast and she leaves. She then returns with a very big bottle. She refills the glasses. The actor-*KING *gooses her heartily with his scepter. She leaps into the air but is extremely flattered. She sashays across the stage proudly displaying all her terrific parts. The actor-*KING *follows her with his burning eyes. Taking advantage of the actor-*KING*'s fascination with* DAGNY BORG, *the actor-*STERNBORG *gets up and follows the actor-*KING*'s head motions exactly. With a small funnel and a bottle of poison, he tries with every move to get some poison into the actor-*KING*'s ear. Eventually, the actor-*KING *starts to "hear" something peculiar. He tries to clean out his ear and finally drops dead. Actor-*STERNBORG *takes the crown off the actor-*KING*'s head and twirls it on his fingers pensively, while looking around for someone to crown.* DAGNY BORG *is busy trying to pry the scepter out of the dead actor-*KING*'s hand. Finally, actor-*STERNBORG *gets the bright idea to put the* *crown back on the head of the dead actor-*KING. *Then both he and* DAGNY BORG *prop the dead actor-*KING *up on the bed, with the crown on his head, as if the bed were a throne. Actor-*STERNBORG *tries to take the scepter from* DAGNY BORG *to replace it in the dead actor-*KING'*s hand, but she's grown very attached to it and hates giving anything back. After some struggle, actor-*STERNBORG *manages to get it away from her and places it in the dead actor-*KING'*s hand. Then both he and* DAGNY BORG *bow to the audience. Applause.*

During the performance, there are various "asides" between STERNBORG *and* EIGHT EYES *about* FORTINBRAS'*s reaction to the events in the play-within-the-play, such as: "Now watch him," "Did you notice anything?", but* FORTINBRAS *only responds to* DAGNY BORG *and doesn't seem to follow the action at all.*]

FORTINBRAS. [*applauding enthusiastically*] Bravo, bravo!

[*The actors bowing a great deal. After they've enjoyed considerable applause, they clear the stage, taking out the bed and the dead actor-*KING.]

FORTINBRAS. She has marvelous tits. Absolutely marvelous. [*to* STERNBORG] What's the play about?
EIGHT EYES. It's a family drama.
FORTINBRAS. Ah. It's going to be a hit. Excuse me, please. I must go tell her what great tits she has.
STERNBORG. [*aside to* EIGHT EYES] He's a complete idiot. Let's make him King.

[STERNBORG *grabs* FORTINBRAS *by the arm as he's about to leave.*]

STERNBORG. Just a minute, Prince. I don't know how to put this.

FORTINBRAS. [*impatiently*] You can tell me but hurry up.

STERNBORG. Your father is ill.

FORTINBRAS. Oh.

STERNBORG. Your father is seriously ill.

FORTINBRAS. [*snapping his fingers*] Faster faster.

STERNBORG. In fact, your father is dead.

FORTINBRAS. Faster faster.

STERNBORG. Wait a second. [*sobbing loudly*] In fact he's been dead for two years. We were afraid to tell you because when your brother Mortinbras found out, he lost his head.

FORTINBRAS. That's it? Can I go now?

[FORTINBRAS *exits.*]

STERNBORG. [*slightly shocked by* FORTINBRAS*'s reactions, he turns to* EIGHT EYES] What do you think?

EIGHT EYES. I'm no expert in theatrical matters, but personally I thought she was second-rate.

Scene 14

[STERNBORG *and* EIGHT EYES *are on stage.* DAGNY BORG *comes running over to* STERNBORG *excitedly.*]

DAGNY BORG. Uncle, Uncle. Prince Fortinbras asked me for my . . .

STERNBORG. I know. I know. He's a fan of your parts.

DAGNY BORG. He asked me for my hand.

STERNBORG. That too? You see. You never know.

DAGNY BORG. He wants to marry me.

STERNBORG. Congratulations. Where but in Norway

could you find such a receptive audience? You will be Queen soon.

DAGNY BORG. That's what he said.

STERNBORG. He's going to be a king.

DAGNY BORG. [*squealing with excitement*] That's what he said.

STERNBORG. Ask him to come in so we can celebrate. What is he doing now?

DAGNY BORG. He keeps pacing back and forth.

STERNBORG. Doing what?

EIGHT EYES. Drinking?

DAGNY BORG. No. Writing.

STERNBORG. Writing what?

DAGNY BORG. A letter.

STERNBORG. A letter?

EIGHT EYES. A letter?

DAGNY BORG. A letter but it's going to be hard to read it.

STERNBORG. A letter to whom?

DAGNY BORG. His handwriting is terrible. Where was he educated?

STERNBORG. [*yelling*] A letter to whom?

DAGNY BORG. To Hamlet. I'm sure he's finished by now. I'll go and get him . . .

STERNBORG. [*interrupts*] Are you sure it's to Hamlet?

DAGNY BORG. Absolutely. I can read.

[DAGNY BORG *dashes offstage.*]

SILENCE

STERNBORG. Well well well. We've got a writer at court now.

[*Sounds of giggling, bodies falling heavily together and then the distinct sound of lovemaking, getting more and more heated as the conversation continues.*]

STERNBORG. What do you think?
EIGHT EYES. I think they're fucking.
STERNBORG. Do you want to listen some more or can we talk?
EIGHT EYES. Just a second.

[*Sounds grow more passionate.*]

STERNBORG. He's too alive to be a king.

[*While* EIGHT EYES *listens eagerly to the climax offstage,* STERNBORG *pulls out an official paper and signs it. As orgasm completes, he hands the paper to* EIGHT EYES *significantly.*]

STERNBORG. Kill him.

VERY   DARK

ACT TWO   Scene 1

[*A long, bloodcurdling howl is heard. Enter* GUARDS.]

GUARD ONE. Who's screaming?
GUARD TWO. Fortinbras.
GUARD ONE. [*indifferently*] Aha.
GUARD TWO. Sternborg condemned him to death.
GUARD ONE. Must hurt. For what?
GUARD TWO. High treason. But he's tough. He's been
    screaming like that for three hours.

[*Screaming stops.*]

GUARD TWO. It's over. Finally!

[FORTINBRAS *crosses stage drunkenly and disappears.*]

GUARD ONE. Wasn't that Fortinbras?
GUARD TWO. Aha!
GUARD ONE. Are you sure he's dead? He looks drunk
    to me.
GUARD TWO. [*thinks*] Well, let me think.

[*Howling begins again.*]

GUARD TWO. [*he's got it*] You know what? Maybe it
    wasn't Fortinbras who was howling.
GUARD ONE. But somebody's screaming.
GUARD TWO. Hold on. Let's listen.
GUARD ONE. It seems to me . . .

GUARD TWO. Shhh!

[*Another howl.* GUARD TWO *listens intently, following howl's melodic line.*]

GUARD TWO. It's Eight Eyes. No doubt about it.
GUARD ONE. [*skeptical*] Well . . . Eight Eyes' voice is much higher.
GUARD TWO. Of course, it's him. Just listen.

[*Another howl, melodically much more complex.*]

GUARD ONE. [*nods*] You were right. It's him.
GUARD TWO. They finally finished off that son of a bitch.

[EIGHT EYES *enters. His hands are bloody and tucked under his belt is something resembling a human face. The* GUARDS *freeze in terror.*]

GUARD TWO. [*yells*] Long life to Eight Eyes.

[EIGHT EYES *smacks the two of them in the face with his bloody hands and leaves.*]

GUARD TWO. You know, I don't think it was him who was screaming.
GUARD ONE. You could be right. But why did he hit you?
GUARD TWO. It's because I yelled.
GUARD ONE. I didn't yell and I got hit, too. What a fucking job!
GUARD TWO. But it pays well.

Scene 2

[FORTINBRAS *and* EIGHT EYES *enter from opposite sides of the stage.* FORTINBRAS *is rocky on his feet and very hung over. He and* EIGHT EYES *see each other.* FORTINBRAS *is scared. He notices* EIGHT EYES's *bloody hands and the strange bundle under his belt.* EIGHT EYES *takes a step forward.* FORTINBRAS *instinctively takes one back.* EIGHT EYES *smiles.* FORTINBRAS *returns the smile.* EIGHT EYES *bursts out laughing.* FORTINBRAS *laughs with him, tentatively.*

EIGHT EYES *extends his bloody hand for* FORTINBRAS *to shake. He hesitates for a second and then grasps* EIGHT EYES's *hand heartily and they shake. Now both of them have blood on their hands.*

EIGHT EYES *goes over to the barrel that* STERNBORG *bathed in. He begins to wash his hands as he talks.* FORTINBRAS *follows.*]

EIGHT EYES. [*washing*] Congratulations, Prince.
FORTINBRAS. [*scrubbing*] What for?
EIGHT EYES. The official death of your father.
FORTINBRAS. Oh, thank you very much.
EIGHT EYES. I mean, you did want to be king, didn't you?
FORTINBRAS. [*staring fixedly at the bulge under* EIGHT EYES' *belt*] What is that?
EIGHT EYES. You mean this?
FORTINBRAS. Yeah. Is that . . . someone?
EIGHT EYES. Oh, him. [*He whips out the skin of Sternborg from under his belt and it unfolds full length*] Ah, you mean Sternborg!
FORTINBRAS. [*takes a swig from his bottle*] Oh yes. Naturally.

[EIGHT EYES *pins the skin to the tree with a dagger.* STERNBORG *seems to be almost alive.* EIGHT EYES *studies the skin close up, as though he were looking at a work of art.*]

EIGHT EYES. He didn't suffer at all. Only two incisions, see? Feet and balls. [*points out the incisions proudly*] Take a closer look.

FORTINBRAS. I can see from here. Nice work.

EIGHT EYES. [*flattered*] Oh, thank you, Prince. See, once I'd flayed him, I put his body on an anthill. And then, I hung the skin on a tree. That's the usual practice, you know?

FORTINBRAS. I know.

EIGHT EYES. I wanted to show him the extent of his errors so that it would serve as a warning to him in the future. And you know, usually, if you put a man in front of his skin he just stares at it.

FORTINBRAS. I can understand that.

EIGHT EYES. But not Sternborg.

FORTINBRAS. [*surprised*] No?

EIGHT EYES. No! He just stared at me the whole time and his eyes were so sad . . . So sad . . . [*They silently examine* STERNBORG's *skin and then* EIGHT EYES *sighs deeply.*]

FORTINBRAS. I can imagine how you felt.

EIGHT EYES. Believe me, Prince. I would rather it was my hide than his. But what could I do? I had to skin him alive in self-defense.

FORTINBRAS. Naturally.

EIGHT EYES. I didn't have any choice. He'd condemned me to death. [*candidly*] Tell me, Prince, how did you find out about your death warrant?

FORTINBRAS. Death warrant? What do you mean?

EIGHT EYES. [*smiling conspiratorially*] Oh Prince. I

know perfectly well that the death warrant was for you.

FORTINBRAS. [*incredulously*] For me?

EIGHT EYES. Of course. I thought it was very smart of you to replace your name with mine. In fact, I am flattered that you considered me. I got your point. Two smart men can always understand each other, don't you think? [*laughs*]

FORTINBRAS. [*laughs*] How did you find out?

EIGHT EYES. [*still laughing*] I read the original.

FORTINBRAS. [*drinks some more*] So if you knew, why didn't you skin me instead of Sternborg?

EIGHT EYES. [*suddenly nervous*] Did I make a mistake?

FORTINBRAS. Ha ha ha. No, no, no. You did very well.

[FORTINBRAS *takes another swig.*]

EIGHT EYES. [*very sincerely*] Thank you, Prince. I think I made the right decision. I had a moment's hesitation, but who was Sternborg after all? A second-generation pig farmer. He was an offense to the Norwegian people. But you, [*very moved*] when I saw the way you talked to Polonius and heard how you dealt with Sternborg's niece . . . then I knew that you had the capacity to be a great king.

FORTINBRAS. Thank you very much.

[*They shake hands, hug, then shake hands again and kiss.*]

EIGHT EYES. I'd better go. Sternborg's friends and supporters are waiting for decapitation and by now they must be getting impatient. I was just going to ask you to sign the warrants.

FORTINBRAS. A big crowd?

EIGHT EYES. Well, not too many. Fifty thousand.

[FORTINBRAS *takes a long swig from his bottle.*]

FORTINBRAS. Fifty thousand?

EIGHT EYES. [*hands him a pen*] Don't worry. One signature is all I need.

FORTINBRAS. [*signing*] He was more popular than I thought.

EIGHT EYES. [*with nostalgia*] A lot of people loved him. Oh, one more thing. I have a daughter.

FORTINBRAS. [*ready to sign the next order*] OK. Give me the warrant.

EIGHT EYES. [*shocked*] No! There is a job opportunity for her. She's fourteen and she's been dreaming of becoming the first woman executioner. You know how these girls are today.

FORTINBRAS. Ambitious.

EIGHT EYES. That's it. The former executioner was very fond of her and often gave her the opportunity to express herself. She was best on the delicate parts like eye gougings, tongue splitting, prick plucking. We now have an excellent candidate for her first job.

FORTINBRAS. Who?

EIGHT EYES. Our secret police, posing as pirates, captured Prince Hamlet . . .

FORTINBRAS. Hamlet! Hamlet is here?

EIGHT EYES. Yes. It was Sternborg's last decision. He invited him here to goose him along a little. Hamlet was supposed to take revenge for his father's death a month ago. He was supposed to kill his uncle Claudius before Laertes does away with him but [*losing control, yelling*] Jesus Christ, this guy is so fucking slow. You know me, Prince. I'm easy but he's driving me crazy. He's asking questions all the time. He's not one hundred percent sure that his Uncle Claudius killed his father. He wants proofs from me! I can't stand him any longer.

FORTINBRAS. [*calming* EIGHT EYES] Calm down. It's not worth getting so upset about.

EIGHT EYES. [*yelling again*] We should just forget all this goddamned diplomacy, finish with him and send in the army. We'll worry about Claudius and the guerillas afterward.

FORTINBRAS. [*takes a long swig from the bottle*] Whatever you say, my friend.

EIGHT EYES. Thank you. One more thing, Prince. I hate to bring this up. It's extremely delicate.

FORTINBRAS. [*nervous*] Yes?

[EIGHT EYES *indicates* FORTINBRAS's *attire with some displeasure.*]

FORTINBRAS. Yes?

EIGHT EYES. Perhaps you could change some of them before the funeral. You know what I mean.

FORTINBRAS. Ah, I see. Absolutely. Good idea.

EIGHT EYES. [*bows gratefully, ready to exit*] Thank you, Prince.

FORTINBRAS. [*points to the skin on the tree*] You forgot your . . . I mean Sternborg.

EIGHT EYES. Oh, yes, indeed!

[EIGHT EYES *takes the skin down carefully and rolls it up, puts it under his arm, and bows as he exits.*]

DARKNESS

Scene 3

[*A huge mirror upstage.* DAGNY BORG, *elegantly dressed, is seated in front of it. Various beauty aids and wigs are spread about her. She remains immobile, her head buried in her hands. Enter* FORTINBRAS, *very drunk, followed by* TWO GUARDS, *one carrying a large basin of water and the other holding a change of clothes.* FORTINBRAS, *with the* GUARDS' *help, begins to wash up and change, taking a long swig from his bottle from time to time.*

He addresses DAGNY *while washing his teeth carefully with his finger.*]

FORTINBRAS. Congratulate me. I killed your uncle. Isn't it great? I saved my skin. Ha ha ha. Yah!

[FORTINBRAS *slaps himself all over.*]

No. It's true. Look at me.

[*Looks to the* GUARDS.]

I look alive, don't I?

[GUARDS *nod that he does, indeed, look alive.*]

[*to* DAGNY] Now we can get married and you'll be queen.

[FORTINBRAS *tries on different shirts.*]

So which one should I wear . . . black?

[GUARDS *nod yes.*]

White?

[GUARDS *nod yes.* FORTINBRAS *gets disgusted with them.*]

[*to* DAGNY] Do you know who's here? Hamlet.

They're going to kill him and I'm not going to help. Awful, huh? [*confidentially*] Did Eight Eyes tell you to change too? You look wonderful.

[*Still changing clothes with the* GUARDS' *help but making it very difficult for them because he's constantly moving as he gets new ideas.*]

[*to* GUARDS] I was sure, I KNEW that Eight Eyes was afraid of Sternborg, that he hated Sternborg and that he'd use any excuse to get rid of him, and I was right.

[GUARDS *nod together.*]

[*proudly*] Listen, Eight Eyes prefers me. He trusts me. He likes me.

[GUARDS *nod in approval.*]

I know what you mean. That's nothing to brag about, huh?

[GUARDS *making ambivalent gestures.*]

Well, he's a killer. I'm an alcoholic. Now that's a ruling body for you. What do you think? Huh?

[GUARDS *nod emphatically.*]

[*to* DAGNY BORG] Say something. I know you hate me because I killed your uncle but I love you.

[GUARDS *make lewd gestures to one another.*]

Maybe you'd prefer if he'd killed me and you'd married him? But you can't marry him because he was your uncle. And besides, he's dead. Wait a second, where was I? Did I tell you I killed your uncle? I didn't. I never did. Well, in a way I did. How do I look?

[GUARDS *nod.*]

No. Give me the other one.

[*He changes his clothes again and eventually washes himself with restraint.*]

[*deeply moved suddenly*] I used to have a little dog.

[GUARDS *are also deeply moved.*]

[*to* DAGNY] He was a little bit shorter than you but he was the one person in the world that I really loved. And he loved me too. Then one day, when I took him for a walk . . . oh fuck it. I never had a dog. I just made it up. I did have a horse but I hung him. But you. I love you. I really love you. [*to* GUARDS *impatiently*] OK. OK.

[GUARDS *finish dressing him by placing a ceremonial helmet on his head.* FORTINBRAS *shoos them out.* GUARDS *exit winking at one another.* FORTINBRAS *draws closer to* DAGNY.]

No, Dagny, really. Don't be mad at me. Please? I hate it when you're mad at me. It makes me want to drink. [*he drinks*] Did I tell you how good you were yesterday? In such a small part. I was so proud of you. I . . .

[FORTINBRAS *strokes her hair and her head falls to the ground with a thud and rolls across the stage.*]

Oh, my God! Oh no.

[FORTINBRAS *smashes the bottle against the wall. Explosion of broken glass.*]

DARKNESS

Scene 4

[HAMLET *is sitting in his cell on a chair with his hands chained behind his back. There's blood on his face.*

FORTINBRAS *enters, dragging a chair along behind him.* FORTINBRAS *sets up his chair in front of* HAMLET. *The two men look at one another. There's a moment of silence.* FORTINBRAS *pulls out a new bottle and takes a swig.*]

FORTINBRAS. So Hamlet, you look terrific. We've met before. It was in Wittenberg. You probably don't remember me. Ach, it doesn't matter. We should talk. Maybe you remember Dagny Borg? This actress? It doesn't matter. Listen, I want you to understand that this is not a-a-a-a-an official conversation. Understand? Excuse me, you have something on your face.

[*Using his own sleeve,* FORTINBRAS *wipes off some of the blood on* HAMLET'*s face.*]

FORTINBRAS. There. Now relax. Why don't you say something?
HAMLET. Greetings.
FORTINBRAS. I'm Fortinbras.
HAMLET. Maybe.
FORTINBRAS. No. For sure. I am.
HAMLET. I didn't say you weren't.
FORTINBRAS. But you didn't say I was.
HAMLET. What difference does it make?

FORTINBRAS. No difference to me. Big difference to you. Have a drink.

[FORTINBRAS *raises the bottle to* HAMLET'*s lips.* HAMLET *desperately flips his head from side to side trying to avoid the bottle.*]

HAMLET. Trying to poison me?

FORTINBRAS. Eh, come on. What's wrong with you? You've become very mistrustful.

[FORTINBRAS *takes a swig from the bottle.*]

HAMLET. It surprises me as well.

FORTINBRAS. But even sober you believed in your father's ghost.

HAMLET. So you know about the ghost too.

FORTINBRAS. I hear things.

HAMLET. Why do you think I believed it?

FORTINBRAS. That's what it looks like, no? Yes?

HAMLET. From a distance, perhaps. But I suspected my father was alive and hiding somewhere, planning a big purge. It was just impossible for me to believe that a scoundrel like Claudius could destroy an experienced assassin like him so easily.

FORTINBRAS. But you saw his corpse.

HAMLET. They showed me a closed coffin. I didn't know who was inside. Also I wasn't sure how much my mother and Claudius were involved. So I tried to wait. I was concerned with the possibility of sudden resurrections. Do you know who Doubting Thomas was?

FORTINBRAS. One of Jesus' friends? Wasn't he the one who couldn't bring himself to believe in the resurrection?

HAMLET. He had doubts not about whether Christ had risen, but how long he had risen for. That's why he was afraid to believe and afraid to disbelieve.

FORTINBRAS. But in the end, he did believe, didn't he?

HAMLET. Who knows?

FORTINBRAS. Of course he did. It's the only reason anyone remembers the stupid guy. So did you finally believe that your father had been killed?

HAMLET. Is it so important? How is your father? I heard that he was very sick.

FORTINBRAS. I heard that, too.

HAMLET. Some people say he's dead.

FORTINBRAS. Is it so important? Actually, he *is* dead.

HAMLET. I'm sorry.

FORTINBRAS. Don't take it too hard. He's been dead for two years.

HAMLET. For two years?

FORTINBRAS. He told me so yesterday.

HAMLET. You drink too much.

FORTINBRAS. Now I'm drinking less because my hands have been trembling so much half of it spills on the ground.

HAMLET. So when are you going to kill me?

FORTINBRAS. Kill you? Don't you understand? I'm trying to save you.

HAMLET. What do you want from me?

FORTINBRAS. I want you to become King of Denmark.

[HAMLET *looks at his chains and smiles at* FORTINBRAS.]

HAMLET. You want me to become the King of Denmark?

FORTINBRAS. [*suddenly nervous*] Don't repeat it. I'm not deaf. Do I look like someone who doesn't know what he's saying? Don't go too far with me. So, what did I say?

HAMLET. You want me . . .

FORTINBRAS. [*angry*] I know! And stop yelling. Someone could overhear us.

HAMLET. [*smiling*] Are you afraid?

FORTINBRAS. No. You are afraid. So do you accept or not?

HAMLET. Is this how they interrogate people in Norway?

FORTINBRAS. Shut up! Yes or no and talk fast because soon I will be too drunk to remember.

HAMLET. Why should I accept?

FORTINBRAS. Why shouldn't you? If you accept you'll survive, if not they will kill you.

HAMLET. Who are "they"?

FORTINBRAS. Claudius and Eight Eyes. Unless you're not interested in saving your own life.

HAMLET. I wonder about that. "To be or . . . "

FORTINBRAS. I know. I know. I've heard all of that. But you can't wonder too long. Yes or no.

HAMLET. Why don't you like my Uncle Claudius? He's an obedient puppet.

FORTINBRAS. Nah, come on! Claudius is finished. He can't deal with the guerillas. You Danes hate him and we don't need him anymore.

HAMLET. How long are you going to need me?

FORTINBRAS. Oh, you? You are something quite different. The people love you. They respect you. You can talk to the guerillas and they will listen to you, right?

HAMLET. Talk about what?

FORTINBRAS. Talk about what. Talk about what. What

do you mean, talk about what? Ask them to be realistic. Ask them to wait. Calm them down.

HAMLET. Calm them down?

FORTINBRAS. Don't repeat it, damn it!

HAMLET. I can only calm them down by giving them what they want.

FORTINBRAS. Oh yeah? You can also calm them down for good.

HAMLET. Yes, YOU can, but that would be a lot of trouble, even for Norway.

FORTINBRAS. Trouble even for Norway. Yak yak yak. All you do is talk. Move! Save your country. Educated asshole. You expect too much. Total independence now is impossible. Eight Eyes will never permit it. Look, Eight Eyes doesn't even want to talk to you. He wants to kill you. I want to help you. What did I say? I need time to gather some strength here. You Danes have to help. It's up to you, for Chrissake! Talk to the fucking guerillas. Convince them. They trust you.

HAMLET. Is that a reason to cheat them?

FORTINBRAS. Cheat them? Save them!

HAMLET. If I understand you correctly, you are asking me to become a collaborator.

FORTINBRAS. A patriot. A patriot! You . . . [*exasperated, he smashes* HAMLET *across the face. Then dabs the blood away again.*] I'm sorry. You've got to understand. You're making me nervous. Don't be so goddamned noble. I'm taking personal risks just coming here. Eight Eyes hates you. Even if you accept my offer I'm not sure how he will react. Listen, I don't want to see your stupid guerillas butchered anymore than you do, but Eight Eyes would love it. If you don't cooperate with me, you'll be killed and one of our agents will take your place, like Laertes, for instance.

HAMLET. Is this the way you spoke to Claudius?

FORTINBRAS. I've never even met him.

HAMLET. Did Claudius really kill my father?

FORTINBRAS. What's the matter with you? Why don't you believe it? What do you want, proof?

HAMLET. Did I kill Polonius?

FORTINBRAS. You saw him lying behind the curtain, didn't you?

HAMLET. Yes, but how long had he been lying there?

FORTINBRAS. How the fuck do I know? Are you sorry for him or what?

HAMLET. I don't trust you. I don't believe a word you say.

FORTINBRAS. Why not?

HAMLET. I don't even have any proof that I'm talking to Fortinbras.

FORTINBRAS. You really are a hopeless motherfucking madman. Too bad.

[FORTINBRAS *opens a new bottle and takes a long drink.*]

HAMLET. Suppose I became King without Norway's assistance and really tried to gain independence for Denmark?

FORTINBRAS. Ha! That would be the shortest insurrection in history. We'd wipe you out in one day.

HAMLET. The Finns would never let you move against us.

FORTINBRAS. [*laughs*] The Finns. Oh please. [*can't stop laughing*] Stop. The Finns. That's a good one.

[FORTINBRAS *tries to get control of himself, trying to catch his breath.*] So yes or no?
HAMLET. No.

[*There's a moment of silence.* FORTINBRAS *gets up and begins pacing the stage, mumbling to himself angrily. All of a sudden he stops in front of* HAMLET *and just stares at him threateningly.* HAMLET *is getting a little bit nervous.*]

FORTINBRAS. Get up. I said GET UP!

[HAMLET *stands.*]

FORTINBRAS. Turn around.

[HAMLET *turns around suspiciously, as* FORTINBRAS *circles him and studies him.* FORTINBRAS *takes off his helmet and hands it to* HAMLET.]

FORTINBRAS. Here. Try it on.

[HAMLET'*s hands are still chained.* FORTINBRAS *removes the chains and hands* HAMLET *the helmet.*]

HAMLET. What for?
FORTINBRAS. Put it on!

[HAMLET *puts the helmet on and then begins rubbing his wrists.*]

FORTINBRAS. Now, the cloak.

[FORTINBRAS *drapes* HAMLET'*s shoulders with his cloak and looks on with satisfaction.*]

FORTINBRAS. Excellent!

[FORTINBRAS *pushes* HAMLET *into his chair, then sits in* HAMLET'*s chair and stares at him.*]

FORTINBRAS. Listen, I have an idea.

HAMLET. Something treacherous.

FORTINBRAS. Shut up. I've got an idea and I don't get too many of them so listen. We look very much alike.

HAMLET. [*offended*] We do not.

FORTINBRAS. Yes. We're the same height.

HAMLET. [*straightens up*] I'm taller.

FORTINBRAS. And around the eyes a bit . . .

HAMLET. [*indignantly*] The eyes . . . ?

FORTINBRAS. OK, so mine are puffy. So what?

HAMLET. I don't find this flattering.

FORTINBRAS. You think I'm a bastard, don't you? [*he lunges like a monster at* HAMLET]

HAMLET. And you think you're an honest man.

FORTINBRAS. Let's change places.

HAMLET. What do you mean?

FORTINBRAS. If you don't want to be King of Denmark, you can be King of Norway instead.

[HAMLET *starts laughing.* FORTINBRAS *also laughs briefly.*]

FORTINBRAS. Have you noticed?

HAMLET. What?

FORTINBRAS. We even laugh the same way. Stop laughing! [HAMLET *takes off the helmet and hands it to* FORTINBRAS.]

FORTINBRAS. No, no! Wait! The King of Norway is the king of the world. Nobody will notice and if they do I'll hang them. Deal?

HAMLET. Amazing.

FORTINBRAS. Amazing? What do you mean by that!

HAMLET. I'm afraid I'm make a pretty poor Norwe-
    gian.
FORTINBRAS. You never know. If we switch places you
    could handcuff me, torture me, slap my face. It's
    every prisoner's dream.

[HAMLET *smiles, amused, and shakes his head.*]

FORTINBRAS. [*screams at him*] Don't lie! I'll take a load
    off your mind. I'll kill your uncle for you. You will
    deal with Eight Eyes and the rest of Norway.
    Great! I'm going to Denmark tonight. I heard that
    you have a terrific theater there.
HAMLET. You don't like being Fortinbras.
FORTINBRAS. Not your business. Listen, we don't have
    a lot of time. Come on. You can give Denmark
    back its independence. What's wrong with my
    idea? The only thing wrong with my idea is that
    you're not drunk. Here. [*hands* HAMLET *the bottle*]
    Drink!
HAMLET. My doctor told me I have a bad liver.
FORTINBRAS. Who told you that? Your who? What are
    you talking about? Tell your doctor that you don't
    need a good liver if you don't accept my offer.
HAMLET. If you really want to change Norway, do it by
    yourself.
FORTINBRAS. Me? Look at me.
HAMLET. I'm looking.
FORTINBRAS. Look at my hands. They're shaking. I
    can't deal with the people. They're afraid of me.
HAMLET. Tell them not to be afraid.
FORTINBRAS. That will lead to panic. Come on.
    Change places with me!

HAMLET. But I like being Hamlet.

FORTINBRAS. These are desperate days. This is no time for egotism.

HAMLET. Is your father really dead?

FORTINBRAS. It's going to be announced tomorrow morning.

HAMLET. What about Mortinbras and Sternborg?

FORTINBRAS. They're both . . . [*makes a cutting motion around his neck.*]

HAMLET. So you really are King of Norway.

FORTINBRAS. Good joke, eh?

HAMLET. Your hands are trembling.

FORTINBRAS. [*looks at his hands, amused*] Hands. Hands are nothing. Of course they are trembling. What do you expect? [FORTINBRAS *takes another bottle and has a long swig*]

HAMLET. Quit drinking.

FORTINBRAS. [*laughing*] Quit drinking! [*to his vodka bottle*] Did you hear that? [*he laughs again, to* HAMLET] She's laughing at you. Listen, drinking was the best idea I ever had in my life. Actually, it was my only idea, until now. How else do you think I got to be forty?

HAMLET. By drinking?

FORTINBRAS. By drinking. A drunkard is harmless. Nobody bothers with drunkards. Everybody trusts them.

HAMLET. I don't trust you.

FORTINBRAS. I knew you'd say that. You are mentally sick. You haven't gotten it. [*triumphantly*] I've cheated all of them. I've been pretending I was an alcoholic since I was twelve. And they bought it!

HAMLET. But you are not pretending. You are an alcoholic.

FORTINBRAS. Ah, well, because you can't pretend about this. That was the only weak point in my plan. Quit drinking! If Eight Eyes saw me without a bottle, he'd slaughter me like that [*snaps his fingers*].

HAMLET. Then, I don't see any reason for living.

FORTINBRAS. And I don't see any reason for dying.

HAMLET. Don't you see that dying is the only honest thing that's left to do in this world?

FORTINBRAS. [*jumps up, incredibly excited, slams* HAMLET *on the back*] See! See! Now you're talking. That's what I love about the real aristocracy. I would never think of such a thing. But you're completely wrong. The world is going to the dogs but we can change it. We two can . . .

HAMLET. [*interrupts*] No we can't.

FORTINBRAS. You're wrong. I was supposed to be dead and I'm still alive. We can change things. Just accept it, you son of a bitch. I beg you. Come on, goddamn it. I'm not right for it. I'm too drunk. I'm too weak. I have lapses of memory. I've developed a fear of my horse. I'm seeing ghosts. Do it, for Denmark, for you, for me. Come on, you've got to switch places with me. PLEASE!

HAMLET. [*hesitating*] Well . . .

FORTINBRAS. We have so much in common. They killed Dagny Borg. They murdered Ophelia. They . . .

HAMLET. [*interrupts, shocked*] What did you say?

FORTINBRAS. [*surprised*] You didn't know?

HAMLET. They told me they'd murder her if I didn't

kill Claudius but I didn't believe them. I thought it was another trick. I didn't believe them and I don't believe you now.

FORTINBRAS. You believe me.

[*There's a moment of silence between them.*]

FORTINBRAS. Don't you want to know who killed her?
HAMLET. I did.

[FORTINBRAS, *like a typical drunk, is suddenly touched, goes to* HAMLET *and tries to comfort him.*]

FORTINBRAS. Come on. Don't talk like that. I know how you feel but it wasn't your fault and you know it. So . . . are you going to help?
HAMLET. [*broken by the news*] The best thing you can do for this world is to blow it up.
FORTINBRAS. [*disgusted*] Eh, now you're talking like a terrorist.
HAMLET. [*finished with him*] Are you going to strangle me by yourself or do you want to call Eight Eyes?

[FORTINBRAS *slaps* HAMLET *hard. Then he takes out pen and paper, signs something hastily and hands it to* HAMLET.]

FORTINBRAS. Show this to the guards. They'll take you to the border. Go back to Denmark.

[HAMLET *examines the documents suspiciously, takes a couple of steps, looks back at* FORTINBRAS, *and then leaves the stage for a second. He reenters and comes over to* FORTINBRAS.]

HAMLET. Thank you.

[*There's no reaction from* FORTINBRAS.]

HAMLET. Listen, Fortinbras. I didn't change my mind
but I want to trust you. I'll go back to Denmark,
kill Claudius, and then we'll talk.

FORTINBRAS. [*passionately*] Don't kill Claudius! That's
exactly what they want you to do.

HAMLET. So what do you want me to do?

FORTINBRAS. Talk to the guerillas. Ask them to wait.
Give me some time and for Chrissake, watch out
for Laertes.

[*They shake hands in a sixteenth-century manner.*]

DARKNESS

Scene 5

[*Ceremonial funeral music is heard.* GUARDS *appear,
dressed in mourning, shouldering, between two poles, the
heavy casket of the King. The shape of the coffin is indeter-
minable because it has a rich drapery hung over it, encoded
with the royal insignia.*

FUNERAL PROCESSION *follows the casket across the
stage. We see* FORTINBRAS, EIGHT EYES, *and several*
MOURNERS *following.*

FORTINBRAS *pulls out a bottle from inside his cloak.
He guzzles it all down in one swig. He turns the bottle
upside down to show the crowd that it's empty. The* MOURN-
ERS *applaud discreetly.*

The GHOST OF FORTINBRAS's FATHER *enters. He
whistles to* FORTINBRAS. FORTINBRAS *turns back and sees
the* GHOST. GHOST *is signaling wildly that he wants to
talk.*]

FORTINBRAS. Daddy, I can't now. I'm busy burying you.

[*The* MOURNERS *in the processional are deeply moved by* FORTINBRAS*'s pathetic cries for his dead father.* EIGHT EYES *is particularly moved and pats* FORTINBRAS *to comfort him.*

GHOST *continues to signal impatiently.*]

GHOST. Fuck them. Come over here.

[FORTINBRAS *leaves the* PROCESSION, *which then exits; but he's hesitant to get too close to his father.*]

FORTINBRAS. What do you want?
GHOST. Get over here!

[FORTINBRAS *goes to the* GHOST *and the* GHOST *slaps his head.*]

GHOST. I hated the way you talked to this Dane. You're a full-blooded Norwegian aristocrat and that's nothing to be ashamed of.

[GHOST *wants to slap him again but* FORTINBRAS *ducks.*]

GHOST. You come from a long line of princes and kings, even a few bishops, before I got sick of them. We may be bloody, but we're still here.
FORTINBRAS. Listen to me.
GHOST. [*interrupts*] Don't interrupt me! We're better than Denmark. That's why we're bigger. Never forget that. You talked to him like a provincial fool and then you let him go. Eight Eyes is furious with you.
FORTINBRAS. But the army loves me.
GHOST. Come on. Be serious.

FORTINBRAS. [*confidentially*] But I've got some help now, Daddy.

GHOST. Help?

FORTINBRAS. Yes. Hamlet.

GHOST. [*incredulous*] Who?

FORTINBRAS. He and I are going to finish off Eight Eyes.

GHOST. [*laughs*] You two will finish off . . . [*he can't stop laughing*] Oh oh oh. I've got to see this. Don't bury me. Stop the procession. You and Hamlet . . . ha ha ha . . . the Killer Princes . . . ha ha ha . . . I can't stand this anymore . . . ha ha ha.

FORTINBRAS. You think you're so smart but they killed you and I'm still alive.

GHOST. Big deal.

FORTINBRAS. What do you know about Hamlet?

GHOST. Eight Eyes has big plans for him.

FORTINBRAS. Plans?

GHOST. Don't repeat it. Now, I'm not saying that I agree with everything Eight Eyes does . . . Dagny Borg, for instance. That was a pity. She had nice tits.

FORTINBRAS. Shut up about her.

GHOST. You are absolutely right, Son. There's plenty of other women. Have you noticed that Eight Eyes' daughter has got lovely hairy legs, like a little deer? When you run your hands down those silky spindles.

FORTINBRAS. What are you talking about? You mentioned some plans. [*yelling*] So tell me. Look, I did what you told me to, Daddy.

[PROCESSION *reenters.*]

FORTINBRAS. [*yelling*] I did everything you asked.

[MOURNERS *exchange sympathetic glances over* FORTINBRAS's *grief.*]

FORTINBRAS. I'm burying you, Daddy.

GHOST. Me? . . . You call that ME? Two years ago, when I was a dying man, I was six and a half feet tall. Now, look at that. Ah ah ah. [*disgusted*]

[GHOST *grabs the drape off the coffin, revealing a small box, with a ribbon tied around it, suspended from the pallbearer's poles.*]

GHOST. And there's space left over!

[GHOST *makes an elaborate gesture of disgust and leaves. Slightly embarrassed, the* MOURNERS *create a line to block the audience's view of the box, as the procession keeps moving.*]

FORTINBRAS. [*yelling after the* GHOST] Daddy! Wait. What plans?

[FORTINBRAS *takes a few more drunken steps toward the procession and then collapses on the stage.*]

Scene 6

[FORTINBRAS *is still lying on the stage when the* WITCH *appears. Paying no attention to* FORTINBRAS *she steps over him. She marks out a circle on the stage. She reaches into her clothes and pulls out some herbs, which she places around the circle. From under her hunch she extracts two smoke pots and sets them up. She begins her incantations, moaning and mumbling.*

GUARDS *enter carrying a big mirror. They step over*

FORTINBRAS *and set the mirror up in the left corner of the stage, its back to the audience.*

Enter EIGHT EYES *carrying a chair. Like everyone else he steps over the Prince and sets up his chair.*

EIGHT EYES *claps and the* WITCH *immediately produces a cloud of smoke. From far off come mysterious sounds. After a moment the sounds become louder and more distinct: heavy breathing, exertion, swords clanging together, voices.*]

VOICE OF HAMLET. One.
VOICE OF LAERTES. No.
VOICE OF HAMLET. Judgment?
VOICE OF OSRIC. Hit! A very palpable hit.
VOICE OF LAERTES. Well again.

[*Sounds of swords clanging again.*]

EIGHT EYES. [*anxiously*] Who hit who?
GUARD ONE. Hamlet was hit.
GUARD TWO. No. Hamlet hit him.
GUARD ONE. No. Hamlet was hit.
GUARD TWO. No. Hamlet hit him . . .
EIGHT EYES. Ah. Shut up. [*yells furiously*] Witch!

[WITCH *nervously tries to calm him down while continuing to manipulate her smoke pots. Suddenly she produces a small explosion which stirs* FORTINBRAS *for a moment.*

At the same time, reflected on the back wall of the stage, we can see the duel scene between HAMLET *and* LAERTES *from Shakespeare's* Hamlet. *The duel is being watched by the Danish court. We can see* KING CLAUDIUS, QUEEN GERTRUDE, LAERTES, *and* OSRIC. *The projection can be done using video techniques: a projection device, from the wings, will reflect a picture through the witch's*

*smoke onto the mirror, which will then be reflected onto the
back wall of the stage, creating a fantasylike film.
The video picture shows the duel continuing.*]

EIGHT EYES. No! It wasn't Hamlet who was hit.

HAMLET (ON VIDEO). [*strikes* LAERTES] Another hit.
What say you?

LAERTES (OV). A touch, a touch. I do confess't.

EIGHT EYES. He'll never get Hamlet like that. What the
hell does he think he's doing, bullfighting? [*demon-
strating* LAERTES'*s fighting style effeminately*] It's a
good thing we've got some wine.

CLAUDIUS (OV). Set me the stoups with wine upon that
table.

EIGHT EYES. Finally, asshole.

[OSRIC (OV) *places two goblets with wine in front of* CLAU-
DIUS. CLAUDIUS (OV) *takes the wine, looks around, then
drops a pellet in. Duel* (OV) *continues.* FORTINBRAS *wakes
up, still drunk, and manages to get into a sitting position.
He looks at the screen and tries to follow the action.*]

EIGHT EYES. [*to* FORTINBRAS] God, all the money we
spent rehearsing that fool Laertes.

FORTINBRAS. [*almost sober*] Laertes? What's going on
here?

EIGHT EYES. Just a little Danish politics, but they're so
bad at it that we had to help.

FORTINBRAS. What do you mean?

EIGHT EYES. You know, to tell you the truth, Prince,
when you let Hamlet go I was furious with you, for
a moment, but now I want to apologize. Of course
you were right. It's much better if Hamlet is killed

in his homeland by his compatriots. We'll take care
of Claudius later on.

FORTINBRAS. I see. Smart. [*gets to his feet*]

EIGHT EYES. Thank you . . . Actually, Hamlet's a sur-
prisingly good swordsman. Look now, this should
be one of his final moves. Ha ha ha.

FORTINBRAS. Ha ha ha.

[FORTINBRAS *suddenly moves behind* EIGHT EYES *and
grips his neck with his forearm while holding a dagger to his
gut with the other.*]

FORTINBRAS. If Hamlet dies I'll kill you.

EIGHT EYES. [*unable to move*] What are you doing? Are
you crazy?

FORTINBRAS. Save him.

CLAUDIUS (OV). [*toasting* HAMLET] Hamlet, here's to
thy health. [CLAUDIUS *drinks*] Give him the cup.

[OSRIC (OV) *takes another goblet of wine from* CLAUDIUS
and hands it to HAMLET.]

EIGHT EYES. [*caught and frantic*] Hamlet's wine is poisoned. I can't do anything.

FORTINBRAS. Change it.

EIGHT EYES. It's too late.

FORTINBRAS. I said change it!

EIGHT EYES. I can't.

[HAMLET (OV) *lifts the wine to his lips.*]

EIGHT EYES. [*yelling desperately*] Don't drink.

FORTINBRAS. [*yelling*] Don't drink.

GUARDS. [*yelling*] Don't drink.

[HAMLET (OV) *hesitates for a moment, then sets the glass down.*]

HAMLET (OV). I'll play this bout first.

[*Everyone on stage heaves a sigh of relief.* HAMLET *and* LA-ERTES *take up their positions again.*]

EIGHT EYES. [*still in* FORTINBRAS's *grip*] Witch, cut it off.

[WITCH *makes some maneuvers and the picture disappears with an electronic whine.*]

EIGHT EYES. [*to* FORTINBRAS] Well, it's all right now. Calm down, Prince. Would you mind releasing my throat? What are you so upset about?

FORTINBRAS. [*tightens his hold*] Get the picture back FAST.

EIGHT EYES. [*choking*] Let's talk.

FORTINBRAS. Get the picture back.

EIGHT EYES. [*choking*] Why? Nothing is going to happen. It's boring. It's over. . . . Guards!

[GUARDS *look at each other. After a short discussion they draw their swords . . . and exit.*]

FORTINBRAS. Witch! Get it back.

EIGHT EYES. [*barely audible*] No.

FORTINBRAS. [*yelling quickly*] YES!

EIGHT EYES. NO!

FORTINBRAS. WITCH!

[WITCH, *confused, gets the picture up again. The Danish court* (OV) *is littered with dead bodies. Only* HAMLET *is still alive, but dying.*]

EIGHT EYES. Shit!

FORTINBRAS. [*to* EIGHT EYES] I knew you wouldn't leave it at that. I knew you'd poison the swords.

HAMLET (OV). [*dying*] O, I die, Horatio. The potent poison quite o'ercrows my spirit but I do prophesy th' election lights on Fortinbras. He has my dying voice.

[HAMLET (OV) *looks straight at* FORTINBRAS. *Then his voice dies out and, finally, the picture goes too.*]

EIGHT EYES. [*quickly*] It's great, Prince. Now we've got Denmark. I'll go there and clean things up for you.

[*Suddenly* FORTINBRAS *releases him by flinging him to the floor.*]

EIGHT EYES. [*persuasively*] Listen, listen, listen. I killed Sternborg for you, right? Calm down, Prince. Calm down. Everything will be fine. I have nothing against you. I will never harm you. Just let me go. I know you're upset, you're hung over, but let me go. Are you upset about the girl? I'm sorry I killed the bitch, OK? [*yelling viciously*] What do you think you're doing, you shit?

[EIGHT EYES *throws some of the herbs from the witch's circle in* FORTINBRAS's *face.* FORTINBRAS *is stunned for a moment.* EIGHT EYES *grabs for the dagger. They struggle.*

EIGHT EYES *gets ahold of the dagger.* FORTINBRAS *grabs his arm but is losing the struggle.* FORTINBRAS *pulls his arm down suddenly, driving the dagger into* EIGHT EYES' *gut.*]

EIGHT EYES. [*looking at his blood, says in disbelief*] Why?

What have you done, Prince? You can't get rid of me. You don't exist without me.

[FORTINBRAS *stabs him repeatedly.* EIGHT EYES' *body falls to the floor.*]

DARKNESS

Scene 7

[FORTINBRAS *enters, dead tired and hung over. He is followed by* TWO GUARDS *dressed ceremonially, wearing helmets with the faceplates down. They all walk forward toward the front of the stage, stepping over the fallen body. The* GUARDS *stand at attention as* FORTINBRAS *addresses the audience.*]

FORTINBRAS. I want to ask you one thing. I want to ask you to trust me. Well, I know it's difficult. You have no reason to. I am my father's son. You hated him and were afraid of him and you were right . . . Now you're probably afraid of me. Well, it's true. I've killed people . . . a few. I drink . . . a lot. Still we have to try. Anyway you have no better choice. Listen, I believe this can be a place where you can say what you think, go to sleep, and in the morning, when the milkman knocks on your door, it will not necessarily be the police. I want to assure you that as long as I'm in power, I'll try to make it so.

[*The* TWO GUARDS *draw their swords and hold them high behind* FORTINBRAS *in a salute. Then they remove their helmets. They have the faces of* STERNBORG *and* EIGHT EYES.]

TWO GUARDS. Long life to Fortinbras, King of Norway
   and Denmark. [*they cheer*]

THE END